ONE IN EVERY FAMILY

DISPELLING THE MYTHS ABOUT
LESBIANS AND GAY MEN

Carole Wardlaw

Basement Press
DUBLIN

© Carole Wardlaw 1994

First published in Ireland in 1994 by
Basement Press
an imprint of Attic Press Ltd
4 Upper Mount Street
Dublin 2

ISBN 1 855941 115

A catalogue record for this title is available from the British Library.

The moral right of Carole Wardlaw to be identified as the author of this work has been asserted.

Cover design: Brian Finnegan
Typesetting: Verbatim Typesetting & Design Ltd
Printed and bound by Guernsey Press Co. Ltd

Contents

Introduction

Most of us are aware of our reaction to the word 'gay', one much in use in our evolving 90s. Most people have an opinion on the subject, and currently homosexuality is attracting a great deal of media attention. While it is true to say that while most people understand the terms 'gay' or 'homosexual', few heterosexuals have any understanding of what it is to live as a gay person in today's society. However, all of us have gay people amongst our relatives and friends. Gay people are a minority in our population, but they are a sizeable minority.

'Coming out' – that is, telling people that you are gay – is a very courageous step for anyone to take. Family members and friends may take the news badly, and can reject the gay person. However, it can also be a difficult experience for the person hearing the news. Homosexuality may conflict with your religious views, or with your personal views. You may find it difficult to accept that your child may not now fulfil many of the hopes and ambitions you had for them.

One in Every Family is an attempt to answer some of the questions which you, as a parent, relative, teacher or friend of a gay person, may have, and to provide you with contacts for any further information you may need. Part One contains answers to many of the common questions about homosexuality. In researching the book, I spoke to various experts to find balanced answers to these questions. For Part 2 I interviewed family members and friends of gay people, as well as lesbians and gays themselves; their own personal accounts of their reactions on finding that their son, daughter or friend was gay or lesbian, and their stories of their own difficulties and feelings and, very importantly, their subsequent relationship with the gay person, are very illuminating, and may be useful to you. Identifying with people who have shared similar life experiences can be of enormous help in breaking out of isolation and confusion. And finally, Part 3 provides you with the contacts you may need, some suggested reading and a glossary.

I would like to thank the many people who gave of their time to help me write this book. I would especially like to thank those who allowed me to interview them for Part 2. Many of these accounts were painful in their retelling, and tremendous courage was shown by all concerned.

I would also like to thank the following people for their expert and valuable contributions: Professor Anthony Clare, psychiatrist, university lecturer, writer and broadcaster; Revd Dudley Cooney, Chairperson of the Dublin Methodist Circuit; Karl Hayden, Director,

Body Positive, Ireland; Kieran McGrath, senior social worker, Temple Street Hospital, Dublin; Dr Mary Murnaghan, Dublin-based GP and lecturer in medicine; Senator David Norris, Joycean scholar, lecturer and politician; Cian Ó Tighearnaigh, Chief Executive, Childline, Ireland; Pastor Terry Price, Cork Baptist Church; Father Maurice Reidy, Professor of Moral Theology, Clonliffe College, Dublin; Kieran Rose, Co-Chairperson of Gay and Lesbian Equality Network, Ireland; and Rosemary Troy, psychologist and co-founder of Childline in Ireland.

Carole Wardlaw
September 1994

PART 1

Answer Me This

IS HOMOSEXUALITY HEREDITARY?

For decades now scientists have tried to determine if genetics is responsible for homosexuality. Many studies have been made on fraternal and identical twins, one or both of whom might be homosexual, but results have been inconclusive or conflicting.

These recent studies have, however, met with great publicity. Some people feel that evidence of a 'homosexual gene' would be a strong argument against discrimination, because it would mean that homosexuality is not a 'perversion' but a natural part of some people's make-up. Many others are anxious about such research, however, because they feel that if it is ever proven that homosexuality is hereditary, tests could be devised to determine whether or not a foetus is potentially homosexual. Prejudice is so strong that there are fears that in some quarters these foetuses could well be aborted.

Other theories, for instance that a certain part of a gay man's brain is the same size as a heterosexual woman's and smaller than a heterosexual man's, have attracted some controversy: some people were concerned that lesbians and gay men could be forced, by families or even the state, to take drugs or have operations to alter this part of the brain. On closer examination this research was found, once again, to be based on very insubstantial evidence. The gay men whose brains had been dissected were very few in number and had all died from AIDS-related illnesses. It could well be that the illnesses they suffered or the drugs they took to combat the diseases might have produced the result that the scientists discovered – and, as in a lot of research, the question of female homosexuality was not considered at all.

Some lesbians and gay men say that they feel that they were born gay, that they always felt 'different'; but then many heterosexuals can claim to have always felt especially called to a particular way of life, be it in music, the religious life or medicine. Can we say that these vocations are entirely dependent on our genes? We are born with many talents, gifts and the potential to develop in many different directions. Sexuality is not merely a physical, chemical reaction; it is one of the ways in which we express ourselves and relate to others and the world around us. To claim that there is one gene which controls our sexuality is simplistic.

Psychologist *Rosemary Troy* says that: 'We are all born from the sexual union of a man and a woman. While we are aware that many people who have married and had children are repressed homosexuals, I am unaware of any compelling evidence to suggest that gay sexuality is genetically transmitted.'

Well-known psychiatrist *Dr Anthony Clare* believes that 'The issue of whether homosexuality is hereditary is still open. I cannot say that it has been answered definitively, and I suppose the answer at the present time is that we just don't know.'

ARE PARENTS TO BLAME FOR HOMOSEXUALITY IN THEIR CHILDREN?

Parents often feel a terrible guilt when they learn of their child's homosexuality, and ask themselves: 'What did I do wrong?', 'Was I not loving enough?', 'Was I overprotective?' No one has proved, and it is doubtful whether anyone can prove, whether homosexuality is caused by nature or nurture. *Dr Anthony Clare* says: 'There is no evidence to show that homosexuality can be attributed to anything the parents do.'

Developmental-psychology theories on the possible causes of homosexuality abound, and many of them are conflicting. Freud declared that the heterosexual woman is a female who has successfully negotiated her initial bond of love and identification for the mother and transferred these feelings into a desire to have her father's baby. Lesbians, according to Freud, remain stuck in love for their mothers. Other psychological theories claim that lesbians are too identified with their fathers. Freud's theories – and others' – have been modified and developed in recent decades but the reasons given as to how and why people develop as homosexuals remain confused and conflicting.

The only thing a parent is responsible for is the wellbeing of their child. If your child is lesbian or gay, it is not your fault. The best thing you can do is to try to accept it and encourage them to accept themselves, because chances are that they are going to be gay or lesbian forever.

IS HOMOSEXUALITY A HORMONAL DISORDER?

Various theories have been proposed to explain the origins of homosexuality. Some researchers give important consideration to the possible hormonal causes of homosexuality.

In a study of male homosexuals, Myerson and Neustadt found a relationship between homosexual behaviour and the amount of sex hormones – androgen and oestrogen – in the blood. However, several factors minimise the importance of an endocrine imbalance. First, not all homosexuals exhibit these imbalances; second, many people who are not homosexuals show these hormonal disturbances; and third, individuals have made changes from homosexual behaviour to heterosexual behaviour without altering this hormonal imbalance.

Psychologist *Rosemary Troy* says that: 'I am uncomfortable with the suggestion that homosexuality is a hormonal disorder. What we need is the sensitivity to allow people to be what they are, and to live and develop their lives in accordance with their own needs.'

Psychiatrist *Dr Anthony Clare* feels that 'the evidence suggests that homosexuality is not a hormonal disorder, although there is some evidence to suggest that there may be differences in foetal brain development of some people who go on to become homosexuals. But the research is in a very early stage.'

IS HOMOSEXUALITY A MENTAL ILLNESS IN NEED OF TREATMENT?

Sometimes a concerned parent will believe that their gay child can be cured, and will arrange for them to see a specialist. However, according to Dr Anthony Clare, 'Homosexuality is not regarded any longer as a mental illness in need of treatment. In 1974, 11,000 American psychiatrists voted on whether homosexuality was or was not a disease. Sixty per cent voted in favour of dropping homosexuality from the disease classification.'

In the early 1970s homosexuality was considered a mental illness and many homosexuals were placed in mental institutions, to be 'programmed' out of their 'deviant' behaviour. It is largely due to the efforts of enlightened individuals and the collective action of lesbians and gay men, such as the American activist group GAA (Gay Activists Alliance) that has led to the removal of the stigma of 'disease' from homosexuality. The psychiatric profession has yet to apologise to the world's lesbians and gays for the stigmatisation, incarceration, lobotomisation, castration, drugging and administration of electric-shock treatment that was done in the name of medical science. However, it has to be remembered that twenty years ago there were many genuine illnesses and conditions which were misunderstood – mental illness first among them. Some people suffering from conditions such as depression or mild schizophrenia were treated very badly by society and locked away in an asylum because at the time it seemed like the best solution.

IS THERE A CURE FOR HOMOSEXUALITY?
No. For some parents this is their first question on learning that one of their children is lesbian or gay. Many lesbians and gay men are still brought to psychiatrists, and sometimes some of this profession will recommend therapies to 'cure' a person of this 'disorder'. Hormone shots and aversion therapy are the favourite recommendations. Aversion therapy works by encouraging the patient to respond in a homosexual fashion to images of their own sex, and

then giving them an electric shock to condition the body against such responses. Very few doctors recommend these medieval practices, primarily because they don't work but also because doctors are becoming increasingly more educated as to the validity of a homosexual way of life.

A person can, of course, learn to change their outward behavioural patterns but psychologists tell us that this training in suppressing our thoughts and feelings results only in severe depression and other psychological disturbances and illnesses.

There are books available which are aimed at helping a person change their sexual orientation from homosexual to heterosexual. Most of these are American publications written from a fundamentalist Christian perspective. The 'cures' they propose are generally lifelong celibacy or heterosexual marriage and children. Celibacy – a life without sex, love and companionship – is a very harsh sentence; and to enter into marriage in the hopes of being rescued from sexual and loving desires for people of your own sex is a rather desperate action, and the potential to cause deep suffering for your spouse and children is very great. The Lesbian Lines in Ireland, UK and Europe (telephone services which offers basic counselling and befriending) have in recent years reported a marked increase of married women calling their numbers. While undoubtedly many of these women might have realised their lesbianism only after marriage, some must have recognised it before.

Social worker Kieran McGrath says: 'Some people believe that it is possible to "cure" sexual orientation. I believe that they are mistaken. What may be possible is to alter a person's sexual arousal patterns, but this is not the same thing. Attempting to cure homosexuality is a futile exercise.'

Sometimes a lesbian or gay man will need help when coming to terms with their sexuality or considering 'coming out'. This is a time when extra support may be needed, perhaps from within the lesbian and gay community in the form of a discussion group, or maybe from a trained counsellor. Today it is easier than ever before for lesbians and gay men to receive guidance and health care from a knowledge-able professional, although it is still possible to fall into the hands of someone who is poorly trained in matters relating to the lesbian and gay community or, worse still, someone who is homophobic – that is, someone who hates lesbians and gay men.

DID SOMETHING HAPPEN IN CHILDHOOD TO MAKE MY CHILD GAY?

Many people mistakenly hold the belief that childhood sexual abuse or trauma can turn someone gay. However, this is obviously not the case: many people who are gay were never abused as children, and many people who were abused are not gay. Like everybody else, gay people come from a wide range of family backgrounds, and like everybody else, they cope with their childhood in their own way.

IS SOMEONE LIKELY TO BE SEDUCED INTO THE HOMOSEXUAL LIFESTYLE BY AN OLDER PERSON?

The Oxford dictionary defines the word 'seduce' as meaning 'to lead astray; to persuade, especially a virgin, to have sexual intercourse'. Many people, gay or straight, experience their first sexual encounter this way. One usually associates this with excess alcohol. Many a woman has been seduced this way, and undoubtedly many a homosexual also. However, it takes much more than a seduction to convince someone to enter a gay lifestyle. It is a decision that can be made only of one's own volition. Most gay people are very aware of this, and would avoid pressurising anyone into this difficult choice.

However, this is a common concern I have come across in counselling parents. Whether a child is heterosexual or homosexual, a large age gap can be a matter for concern; but the choice to lead a gay lifestyle is not one that anyone is coerced into.

IS HOMOSEXUALITY JUST A PHASE?

This is a common question. Because of the fear and taboo surrounding homosexuality, people often try to avoid accepting a lesbian or gay man in the vain hope that their homosexuality will simply go away.

One of the strangest clichés in recent years is that homosexuality is 'fashionable'. Lesbians and gay men run the risk of losing their children, families, friends and jobs by being open about who it is that they love. To say that homosexuality is fashionable demeans the lives and loves, the bravery and courage of lesbians and gay men, suggesting that their strongest passions and convictions are whimsical and superficial and not as 'real' as heterosexuals'. It is true, however, that many young people go through a stage of experimentation. Some may have relationships with members of their own sex and go on to be predominantly heterosexual; many others may have relationships with the opposite sex and go on to be gay. But once someone is sure of their own orientation, it is highly unlikely that it will change.

WHAT DIES THE BIBLE SAY ABOUT HOMOSEXUALITY?

The Bible says much less than many religious people would have us believe. The Bible is a book, written by many people and translated several times, and so is open to interpretation, and all Christian denominations differ in their interpretations. For example, teaching on baptism varies from church to church. The Bible passage most frequently taken as evidence to support the position that God denounces homosexuality is Genesis 19; 4-11, which recounts the story of two angels who visit the city of Sodom and stay with Lot.

4: But, before they lay down, the men of the city, the men of Sodom, compassed the house round, both old and young, all the people from every quarter.

5: And they called unto Lot, and said unto him: Where are the men which came in to thee this night? Bring them out unto us, that we might know them. (King James Bible.)

'That we might know them' has been interpreted to mean having sexual knowledge. Lot tries to get the populace to take his two daughters, 'which have not known man' and says:

'Let me, I pray you, bring them out unto you, and do ye to them as is good in your eyes: only unto these men do nothing; for therefore came they under the shadow of my roof.'

At the end of this short Biblical chapter, after the cities of Sodom and Gomorrah have been destroyed by 'brimstone and fire from the Lord out of heaven', we learn that Lot's daughters made him drunk and had sex with him so that they might 'preserve the seed' of their father.

'37: And the first-born bore a son, and called his name Moab: the fame is the father of the Moabites unto this day.
38: And the younger, she also bore a son, and called his name Ben-ammi: the fame is the father of the children of Ammon unto this day.'

So this odd chapter of the Bible, which documents the story of a man who puts the ease of his house guests before the fate of his daughters, daughters he later makes pregnant, is read as evidence that God punishes homosexuality. There is no mention in this passage of lesbians and indeed if we read further in the Bible in the Book of Ezekiel 16: 49-50, we are told that the sin of Sodom was not male homosexual lust but 'pride, surfeit of food, and prosperous ease, neglecting to aid the poor and needy' [Revised Standard Version].

In the New Testament the passage that is used to denounce homosexuality consists only of the words of the apostle Paul and does not relate to anything that Jesus said. Romans 1; 26-27 is where Paul refers to homosexual acts, but it is the idolatry of the Gentiles and their worshipping of false gods that he is condemning. It has to be understood that in Biblical times there was a great deal of idol worship and fertility cults, all sorts of sexual practices.

Jesus himself said nothing whatsoever about homosexuality. He did say 'You shall love the Lord your God with all your heart, with all your soul, and with

22

all your mind. This is the great and first commandment. And the second is like it; you shall love your neighbour as yourself. On these two commandments depend all the law and the prophets' [Matthew 22; 37-40].

There has been a great deal of conflict in recent years between the fundamentalist Christian churches and the lesbian and gay community, built on the fundamentalist assumption that homosexuality and Christianity are completely opposed. However, many lesbians and gay men have a very strong faith and feel hurt, abandoned and punished by their religious institutions when what they would really like is to be embraced, included and loved. As a result of this religious dilemma, many lesbians and gay men have had to form their own place of worship within the Lesbian and Gay Christian movement. This is not an ideal solution and can only add to the ghetto mentality which many lesbians and gay men are forced to adopt, but it is less hurtful than remaining alone and isolated due to the rejection by the larger Christian institutions.

Many churches of all denominations are now taking a fresh look at how they can move forward to a position of dialogue with the lesbian and gay community. It is only a recent happening within the established Christian churches, and has not yet reached the Roman Catholic Church, where women are not yet recognised and allowed to take their rightful place within the church structures. Taking down the barriers with regard to homosexuality will take a while longer.

In order to address this question I discussed this matter with three Christian clergymen: Revd Dudley L. Cooney, Chairperson of the Dublin Methodist Circuit;

Pastor Terry Price of Cork Baptist Church; and Father Maurice Reidy, Professor of Moral Theology at Clonliffe College in Dublin. Here is what they had to say:

Revd Dudley L. Cooney: 'A few years ago the Methodist Council in Ireland passed a ruling saying that gay relationships were acceptable, and the practising of gay sex was also acceptable, provided it was practised within the confines of a stable, lasting relationship.

'However, subsequently the conservative sector within the Council had this changed back to saying that lesbian and gay men were acceptable, but gay practices were not. In my opinion I think that rank-and-file Methodists would be much less hostile to gay relationships than one might expect.

'It has to be understood by people today that the Biblical concept of sexuality has greatly changed with the knowledge we have in our times. For example, it is no longer held that a homosexual man is actively denying life via procreation. Similarly, it is no longer held that women's primary function is childbirth.'

Pastor Terry Price: 'In my own church a gay person could attend services but membership would not be open to them. We would see a gay couple as committing fornication, which we would see as being wrong. In our church the sacrament of communion is a personal thing, so it would be the choice of the individual to partake or not. However, if two people were living in an openly gay relationship, then they would be asked not to take the sacrament. If a gay couple felt that they had to leave my church, I would visit them and try to explain the position of the church to them. There is still a stigma attached to gay people within the church; an unmarried mother would be more readily accepted. I would say that there is still fear and ignorance about lesbians and gay men, and maybe the church needs to do something to remedy this situation.'

Father Maurice Reidy: 'The Catholic approach to homosexuality would be more a matter of conscience, being guided by the Bible, culture, psychological theory and so on. It's not simply a case of what the Bible does or does not teach. In the Catholic tradition, the Bible and the Church teachings form two strands which are of equal importance.

'Homosexuality is not condemned by the Catholic Church. It would be more correct to say that the Catholic Church would see the act of heterosexual *intercourse* as wholesome, and that we would not see other sexual acts in the same way.

'Presently our culture in Ireland is moving towards a greater acceptance of homosexuality. The Church needs to move forward with the cultural changes, but we must also continue in the traditions of the Catholic church. Generally speaking a gay couple would be accepted within the Catholic community. They would be accepted as people, but their sexual practices would not be accepted.

'It is important to point out that the Church has her ideals but that the Church is also made up of human beings, and when we are dealing with humanity, we need to appreciate that there are many shades of grey between black and white. I would say that whether you are heterosexual or homosexual, you can be a saint.'

There are religious organisations specifically catering to gay members. The Metropolitan Christian Church caters to lesbians and gay men and has congregations all over the USA. The American Lesbian and Gay Catholic congregation is known as Dignity; in Ireland and Britain there is Reach, the Gay Christian group, and The Julian Fellowship, the Lesbian Christian Fellowship. More details are to be found in Part 3 of this book.

If parents have religious beliefs which would resolutely reject homosexuality, or if they are 'set in their ways', a son or daughter is less likely to want to upset matters by telling their parents that they are gay. If you disagree with homosexuality on religious grounds, try to accept your child for him- or herself. Their homosexuality is just a part of their personality. Don't pass on the chance to show love and friendship, because that is all that is asked of you.

DO HOMOSEXUALS MOLEST CHILDREN?

Childline was established in Ireland, the UK and Europe as a telephone helpline for children who have been abused in any way, or who simply need to talk to someone about any life situation. The present director of Childline in Ireland is *Cian Ó Tighernaigh*, who has this to say: 'The vast majority of sex-abuse cases are committed by heterosexual men, but some homosexuals have abused as well. But it is not a matter of sexuality. Child sexual abuse is not sexually driven. It is about power and violence. The abuser wants most of all to feel that he has power over the victim. Research has shown that paedophiles are mostly heterosexual men.'

Most child victims of abuse are abused by a person known to them, generally a heterosexual male – generally a father, uncle or brother.

Despite these facts, some people still abhor the idea of lesbians and gay men working with children. There are many lesbians and gay men working as teachers and youth leaders but they keep their homosexuality to themselves. Many lesbians and gay men are afraid of losing their jobs, or of an outcry from parents if their sexual orientation was public knowledge. This is a huge pressure on lesbians and gay men working with children, who, like their colleagues, are usually very committed to the young people in their care.

It is time for society to look at these issues in a more realistic manner. The evidence clearly shows that lesbian and gay men are, in all likelihood, not child abusers and that they have no desire to cultivate an interest in homosexuality in children, either their own or other people's.

Dr Anthony Clare is quite definite in his opinions: 'Homosexuals do not molest children. There is no relationship between paedophilia and homosexuality.' *Rosemary Troy* believes that 'homosexuals as well as heterosexuals can abuse their sexuality and the sexuality of others, can lack sexual boundaries and can abuse the power they have over children in their environment. However, the vast majority of cases I have dealt with in the area of child sexual abuse have been male and female victims of heterosexual men. To classify homosexuals as a threat to children is unfair and ignores the facts.'

Is it wrong for a gay person to bring up a child?
Some lesbians and gay men are bringing up children, usually because they have had children from a previous marriage or heterosexual relationship. In general these are all normal, happy, healthy children. Their parents are not bringing them up to be

homosexual; they are simply, like all parents, rearing their children the best they can.

Some children are brought up with two gay 'parents', either because one partner has children from a previous relationship or in some cases because a lesbian couple have decided that they wanted children and used artificial insemination or a male friend. However, this is not a decision taken lightly – and will a child brought up with love by two women who have thought long and hard about the decision be worse off than a baby conceived in a one-night stand and brought up in poverty?

Some lesbians and gay men feel that they really want children, and feel that they can offer a child a very good and secure life. It used to be argued, and still is by many, that children need to be brought up by two parents, a mother and a father, and that lesbians and gay men should not have children, because there would not be the equal balance of a maternal and paternal role. However, these days many people, for a variety of reasons, are bringing up children on their own, and doing it very well.

The sexual orientation of a person has no bearing on their ability to bring up children. A central issue in many countries at the moment is the right of gay couples to adopt children. This is a very contentious issue, but any person wishing to adopt a child is screened thoroughly – babies are not handed over to just anybody, and rightly so.

WHAT IS THE GAY COMMUNITY?
Many people know that there are such things as gay bars, and they may also be aware of the existence of a

Gay Switchboard or helpline. However, there is much more available for gay people than just a telephone number and a place to go for a drink. Gay people may be interested in politics, especially in helping to improve the standard of life for gay people. In most countries, there exists some kind of gay political group striving to see changes made in legislation, conditions at work, and so on. There are gay people working with AIDS patients and their families. They are involved in promoting safe-sex campaigns, counselling and helping people who are HIV-positive. There are also discussion groups available for people who are just coming out and who perhaps have had no previous contact with the gay community. There are parents-enquiry groups, set up to support and inform parents of gay children. These are often a very important link for parents who are finding it difficult to come to terms with their child's sexuality, or who need to ask questions and to discover that they are not the only parent with a gay child. Many universities and colleges have lesbian and gay societies, where gay students can meet and discuss life on campus, as well as their own personal experiences. There are gay youth groups, like any other youth club, except that all the members are gay. There are also gay bookshops, or certainly bookshops which stock gay literature. There are likewise restaurants which have a predominantly gay clientele. Finally, there are, of course, gay bars and nightclubs. They may be used as pick-up places, but then so are many 'straight' bars and nightclubs. More often, though, these are places where gay people can go to for a drink and a chat with friends, where nobody is going to glance sideways at two men or two women holding hands. On a wider scale, there are gay festivals, such as Gay Pride Week, which marks an historical event (known as Stonewall) 25 years ago, where gay people first started to stand up and be counted. There are any amount of holiday companies and destinations to suit gay people. There are the Gay Games, just like the Olympic games, but where most of the competitors are gay.

Not all gay people become involved in all of these activities or even any of them. However, they are there, and people can dip into them if they wish to do so.

Also, there are many gay and lesbian newspapers and magazines to keep people informed about what is happening in the gay community. All of these groups and helplines have been established to benefit directly the gay community. Gay people have an entire sub-culture which is necessary for their wellbeing and support. Life as a minority puts many pressures on gay people, and so the gay community is important as a resource and social centre for gay people and the parents and friends of gay people who may need their own support and advice.

A list of support groups for gay people and their families can be found in Part 3 of this book.

Is Homosexuality Illegal?

In most places in the world *being* a lesbian or gay man is not a criminal offence but the freedom of lesbians and gay men to live, love, work, rear children, bear arms for their country and have conjugal rights varies greatly depending on the state they live in. The rights automatically conferred with heterosexual marriage – rights of inheritance, adoption, ownership of property, insurance, pension and work benefits, prison visiting, consultation in hospital, citizenship – cannot be readily claimed by lesbian and gay men, no matter how long or how loving their partnership.

The combined countries of Europe have a population of about of 820 million people. Of this total an estimated 50 to 100 million are predominantly or exclusively lesbian or gay. Almost every European country has, at some point in its history, decreed a total ban on homosexuality. In most cases the ban applied solely to sex between men. Six countries also once had a complete ban on lesbianism: Austria, Bulgaria, Czechoslovakia, Finland, Hungary and Sweden. Today, the overwhelming majority of European countries have at least partially legalised same-sex relationships. Nine countries that have repealed the complete ban on homosexual contacts still have an age of consent which is higher for homosexuals than for heterosexuals. Lesbian and gay partnerships are officially recognised in Denmark and Sweden, with other European countries presently considering legislation that would enable lesbian and gay partners to have the equivalent of civil marriage. Membership of the armed forces is open to homosexuals in 12 countries.

Lesbians and gay men in Australia and New Zealand are well protected by legislation. These countries are currently considering recognising lesbian and gay partnerships for the purpose of awarding immigrant visas. The legal situation for lesbians and gay men in the USA varies vastly from state to state: Hawaii has just recognised lesbian and gay couples' rights to civil marriage, while many of the southern states still have laws that criminalise lesbians and gay men.

In Ireland male homosexuality was decriminalised in 1993, and lesbians and gay men, like heterosexuals, are now recognised to be sexually consenting adults at age 17. Though male homosexuality was officially a criminal offence until 1993, no person was ever actually charged with this crime, although there have been many incidents of gay-bashing in Ireland and also threats of blackmail and intimidation. Though homosexuality is perfectly legal in Irish society and lesbians and gay men are protected under the Incitement to Hatred Act, some prejudice remains. However, Ireland was one of the last places in Europe to decriminalise homosexuality, and certainly lesbians and gay men have become much more widely accepted in Ireland since decriminalisation.

It is interesting to compare the legal status of lesbians and gay men in a few of Europe's larger countries to get a better sense of the issues involved and to notice how, with the exception of the UK, there is a general movement, accelerated in recent years, towards a full integration of lesbians and gay men into the civic and public life of Europe's nations.

Denmark: the total ban on male homosexual acts was lifted in 1930, though it was not until 1976 that a common age of consent of 15 was finally introduced. In 1987 the government passed an anti-discrimination statute which protects lesbians and gay men from discrimination in the provision of public services and access to public facilities. The Danish Registered Partnership Act (1989) allows same-sex couples to register their relationship and receive official recognition and legal entitlements on a par with a heterosexual marriage. The only exception is they may not jointly adopt children. Since 1979 homosexuals have been allowed to join the armed forces.

France: prior to 1791 there was a prohibition on

male homosexuality. In 1942 the age of consent was set at 21 for gay men. In 1982 the age of consent for gay men was lowered to 15 in line with the age for heterosexuals. Anti-discrimination laws were introduced in 1985. These protect both lesbian and gay individuals from discrimination in employment and access to goods and services. Homosexuality is not a barrier to membership of the armed forces.

Italy: homosexual acts between men were decriminalised by the Italian state in 1889. In that year, a common age of consent of 14 was introduced for people of all sexualities with the understanding that sex with a 14-to-16-year-old can be punishable if the younger person is 'sexually innocent' and 'morally pure', and if they make a complaint to the authorities. There is no explicit recognition of lesbians nor of partnerships. However, in an attempt to give legal rights to unmarried heterosexual couples the Italian government also inadvertently opened the door to the de facto legal recognition of lesbian and gay couples when it issued new regulations for municipal registration and record offices in 1989. These defined a family as 'a group of cohabiting persons tied by bonds of affection' and did not specify that the partners have to be of the opposite sex.

The Netherlands: the total ban on male homosexuality was lifted in 1811. There had been no age of consent for 100 years when in 1911 the minimum age was set at 18 for heterosexuals and 21 for gay men. Since 1971 the uniform age of consent for heterosexuals, lesbians and gay men has been 16. Though the legal system doesn't give specific recognition to lesbian and gay partnerships, homosexual couples can draw up a legal contract which gives them many of the rights of married heterosexual people, such as property, taxation, and next-of-kin visiting rights in hospitals and prisons. However it excludes child adoption and social-security benefits. Since 1974 homosexuality has not been a bar to membership of the armed forces. Political asylum has also been granted to homosexuals facing persecution in their countries of origin. The national lesbian and gay group in the Netherlands is the oldest in the world, having existed continuously for over 80 years.

Russia: soon after the Bolshevik revolution in 1917 the Tsarist anti-homosexual laws were scrapped. However, in 1934, Stalin recriminalised gay male sex and purged homosexuals from the Communist party government and armed forces. Stalin's legal proscriptions remain in force today. Article 121 of the penal code states that anal intercourse between men is a criminal offence punishable by up to 5 years' hard labour; 880 gay men were arrested under this Article in 1988. During the 1970s there was considerable repression of homosexuals; lesbians and gay men were sometimes blackmailed into working for the KGB and aversion therapy was a common treatment. In 1989 the first gay personal adverts appeared in the Soviet press. For several years there have been informal groups of lesbians and gay men in some of the larger cities. The lesbian and gay community in Moscow were instrumental in defeating the attempted coup of 1992; their publishing press and organisational structure firmly supported Yeltsin.

Spain: male homosexual acts by those 12 and over have been lawful since 1822, with the exception of the years between 1828 and 1932. During the Franco regime from the late 1930s to the late 1970s the public morality laws were often used against gay men. These were repealed in 1978. Today the age of consent continues to be 12 for heterosexuals and homosexuals alike. Since 1984 it has been legal for homosexuals to belong to the armed forces providing sexual contact do not take place in barracks or during duty hours.

United Kingdom: while lesbianism has never been an offence under British law, male homosexual relations were completely illegal in the United Kingdom until the 1967 Sexual Offences Act which decriminalised homosexuality between consenting adult men in private, in England and Wales. This was extended to Scotland only in 1980, and to Northern Ireland in 1982. These laws do not apply to those serving in the armed forces and the merchant navy.

British law offers lesbians and gay men no protection from discrimination. Therefore it is legal to discriminate against gay people in employment, housing, education and the provision of other public and private services. Lesbians and gay men have no protection against incitement to hatred. The foreign partners of British lesbian and gay men have no right to immigrate and stay in the United Kingdom with their partner even if they are in a long-term relationship. In the United Kingdom the law does not recognise long-term gay relationships. A legacy from the Thatcher era means that there is no place in any school, in any circumstances, for teaching which can be interpreted as advocating homosexual behaviour, which presents it as the 'norm' or 'which encourages homosexual experimentation by pupils'. Local authority funding is prohibited from being spent on concerns that might be seen to be 'advocating' homosexuality – generally anything which gives a positive view of gay life. A recent attempt to bring the homosexual age-of-consent laws into line with those for heterosexuals failed in the House of Commons. Some good news for the lesbian and gay community came recently in the form of a ruling from a judge who found that a lesbian mother's partner had the right to be considered as a co-parent.

There may be a great deal of progress in many countries for homosexuals, but there are many more issues which need to be honestly addressed. But as our societies become more educated and informed about the lives of lesbians and gay men prejudice about homosexuality is rapidly decreasing. The cogs of change in society often take a long time to turn but turn they do.

CAN LESBIANS AND GAY MEN BE FIRED FOR BEING GAY?
The answer to this question again depends on the employment laws of the country in which they live. Most European countries have laws prohibiting discrimination against lesbians or gay men in the workplace but in order to fight discrimination lesbians and gay men must be prepared to be absolutely public about their sexual orientation, and that is a luxury and privilege that only the lucky and brave can afford to claim. Lesbians and gay men are often afraid that their colleagues will shun them for fear of being seen to be too closely associated with a 'known homosexual'. It is very uncomfortable situation to find yourself in a situation where same-sex colleagues are hesitant in your company for fear that any sign of friendship might be interpreted in a sexual way.

A great deal can be done to make the workplace a

safer and happier place for lesbian and gay colleagues. In 1987 the Irish Congress of Trade Unions issued very useful guidelines for lesbian and gay rights in the workplace, and these can be found in Part 3.

Do lesbians hate men?

This is a widely held view, but in general lesbians do not hate men, and men do not hate lesbians!

However, some lesbians, as heterosexual women, may have had bad experiences with men, such as an alcoholic or abusive father, or even incest or sexual abuse. This behaviour naturally diminishes these women's trust in men. Indeed, many straight women have lived through these extremely traumatic events, and may have grown to dislike men as a result.

Some lesbians do fall into the category of 'ardent radical feminists', and again, any women, straight or lesbian, with these beliefs can be inclined to statements such as 'I don't need men in my life – I'd much rather live without them'. But not all lesbians are feminists, and not all feminists are lesbians.

However, in general lesbians can have very good relationships with men, because the boundaries are different. A gay woman may feel quite safe talking to a man, because both parties know and understand that there can be no sexual undertones, and both parties are safe in the knowledge that neither party is looking for sex. Simply knowing that this is a good healthy friendship can take a huge amount of pressure off people.

I spoke to one lesbian, who told me: 'I am a lesbian, and I don't hate men. I don't know any lesbian who would say that she hates men. I have some very good friends who are men, some gay men, some straight. I don't really see my friendships divided by gender. I look upon my friends for who they are – I don't see male and female. I don't see myself as trying to be a man either. I'm quite happy being a woman. I don't like to dress all feminine, but that's just because I can't stand lace and bows, and that kind of thing. I dress casually but always smart, I hope. I don't think that lesbians should only stick to their own company. I like to sit in a bar and have a drink with some of the guys as well. They are good company. I certainly don't believe that all men are bastards – some of them are of course, but some women can be real bastards too.'

Gay women have fathers, uncles, brothers, grand-fathers. They have been brought up with men in their lives, and on the whole will have had healthy relationships with these men. Many girls grow up with a close relationship with their father and brothers in particular. It is not true that just because a woman isn't sexually attracted *to* men, she has a problem *with* men.

Is Homosexuality a Lonely Life?

Many parents are worried that their child is going to have an unhappy and lonely life, perhaps without all that they themselves have taken for granted: marriage, children, their own family. When a heterosexual couple gets married or engaged, it is a big occasion: parties and gifts are showered on them, and the social occasion brings happiness to many people. In contrast, when a gay couple commit to each other, there is no big announcement or ceremony, no congratulations or gifts. It is a very private and almost secret matter and this can be very painful – it is natural when you are in love to want to share your feelings with friends and family.

The situation has improved a great deal in recent years, but life must have been appallingly lonely in the past when our society were in deep denial about lesbian and gay sexuality. It is not easy to meet partners where gayness is still considered abnormal and false stereotypes prevail. There is still a large body of opinion which would seem to suggest, falsely, that gay people have no sexual boundaries and want to seduce everyone they come into contact with. We all know of famous characters who lived in lesbian or gay relationships until death parted them, and many lived out their lives in faithful relationships. It is a myth to believe that gay relationships are made up only of one-night stands and short, traumatic relationships. There are those who are unfaithful and even promiscuous, but this is also true of the heterosexual population. A gay person has the same odds as a straight person when it comes to the love stakes. Some will remain single, some will have failed relationships, and many will have long-term relationships in which to grow old.

However, there is no doubt that life can be very lonely at times for gay people. If a gay person has not come out, they will have to lead a double life, being seen to conform to a heterosexual lifestyle and showing at least a passing interest in the opposite sex. If a gay person has not come out, the whole gay community, which can be very supportive, can be closed to them, adding to their isolation. Gay people may also be lonely because they may be living in rural areas with no gay community. There has been a movement within the gay community towards setting up groups in an attempt to break such isolation.

Many people also experience isolation in the

workplace, where gay people are often the butt of jokes or are discussed in disparaging terms. Not surprisingly, many people find that it is better to be a loner than the subject of ribald and offensive 'humour'.

For a single gay person, making friends or finding partners can be difficult. It's hard for anyone, gay or straight, to enter a nightclub on their own. Alternatives include putting an ad in the gay press, but again, this does not suit everybody. And, like many people living in isolation, gay people may be driven by loneliness to drinking or to drugs.

Dr Mary Murnaghan: 'Homosexuality is a lonely life for many due to prejudice, ignorance and the need for secrecy. It must be very difficult to go into work on a Monday morning and say nothing about what a good weekend you had with your friends or partner. These are the topics of conversation in most places of work, and can be the dread of most lesbians' or gay men's lives.

'Some lesbians and gay men lose out on their relationships with family members and friends when they do come out, and this is another aspect of loneliness. It is the most natural thing in the world to want to share our lives, and the people in our lives with our own families especially. Unfortunately, some gay people have been asked to leave the family home, or have been abandoned by their families when they have tried to share their true self with the family. This makes a person think that they must be very bad, if their own family doesn't want to know them. This estrangement from a family can cause, and has caused, some lesbians and gay men to develop severe depression, and even reach the stage of having a severe nervous breakdown.'

Senator David Norris: 'I would say that a gay lifestyle

is not a lonely life. A gay person can meet people at gay gatherings, gay bars, social groups and so on. Gay relationships last equally as long as heterosexual relationships. This in itself is quite amazing considering there are so many pressures on gay couples. Society is against them, the church is against them, their families may be against them, and so on. It takes a very strong relationship indeed to withstand all of these pressures.

'It has to be said that heterosexual relationships are deteriorating very badly in the marriage stakes these days. There appears to be a huge increase in the divorce rate for heterosexual couples, so I don't think that lesbian and gay couples are doing too badly.'

Karl Hayden: 'I know a good number of gay relationships that have been going for many years. In one particular case I know of a couple that have been living together for over thirty years. Both men are in their early sixties. In my experience, where gay people are living a lonely life there is usually a reason. For example, some gay people live a double life. Where this happens I have usually found that the strain causes a person to shut off from people around them. So to say that being gay causes a person to be lonely is more based on the world around them and the prejudice of the heterosexual world than to do with the unhappiness of being gay.'

HOW LIKELY ARE HOMOSEXUALS TO DIE OF *AIDS*?

On a world-wide scale 75 per cent of people with AIDS are heterosexual. It is not a 'gay plague'.

AIDS stands for Acquired Immune Deficiency Syndrome. If someone is infected with the HIV virus they may, in time, develop AIDS. The HIV virus can only be contracted through an exchange of bodily fluids. Nobody dies of AIDS itself but people with AIDS might, however, succumb to disease or infection that their failed immune system cannot overcome. Many gay men have died from AIDS-related illnesses or are currently HIV-positive but due to extensive education of how to prevent the spread of AIDS and to remain healthy with HIV, the rate of infection and fatalities within the gay community has notably decreased in recent years. Sadly, the same cannot be said for the world's heterosexual population.

Tragically, many people with AIDS today find themselves abandoned in hospital wards, or in empty houses. The disease is a long, slow process, but it is an illness, just like any other. It is not something to be ashamed about. Thankfully, many families and friends of gay people are very supportive when faced with AIDS.

Many people still have an irrational fear of catching AIDS. You cannot catch AIDS from casual contact such as shaking hands, hugging, coughing or sneezing. You cannot catch it from a swimming pool, a restaurant, toilet seats or telephones.

If you are concerned about AIDS, or if someone you know is HIV-positive, take the time to talk to one of the telephone helplines listed in the back of this book. The people running these services will be able to provide you with information.

Dr Mary Murnaghan: 'Two hundred people have died of AIDS in Ireland [August 1994]. This means that there is more chance of a person being killed in a road accident than of him dying from AIDS. Only a small percentages of gay men will die from AIDS. The gay community is probably much more educated about practising safer sex than the rest of society. Gay people have been connected with raising awareness around AIDS for years now and they are the front of the line when it comes to practising safer sex and working with people with AIDS.'

I KNOW SOMEONE WHO'S HIV-POSITIVE OR WHO HAS AIDS, AND I DON'T KNOW WHAT TO DO.
Because of popular beliefs and attitudes about HIV and AIDS, someone coping with the disease has also to face a barrage of ignorance and possible rejection by family and friends. The most important thing you can do is to be supportive.

It helps to start by looking at your own feelings. You may be shocked and angry. You may be overwhelmed by sadness, and fearing the loss of someone close to you. However, your willingness to stand by your loved one is the best thing you can offer. Remember that fear grows from ignorance, and the more you know about AIDS and HIV, the more you will be able to cope.

When a person has HIV, they may not develop AIDS for many years, and the uncertainty of the future is a great strain. Coming to terms with a diagnosis of HIV is very difficult indeed. Once the immediate shock is over, many people are determined to fight the virus: eating well, moderate exercise and stress reduction are all positive steps, as are support groups and counselling.

If you are living with someone who is HIV-positive it is important to realise that it is a very difficult virus to catch. Read the above section again for more advice if you need it, or ring one of the helplines listed in Part 3. The main precaution to take is to avoid contact with blood or bodily secretions. Do not share toothbrushes or razors, and stained clothing and linen should be washed on the hot cycle for at least ten minutes. Any breaks in the skin should be covered with waterproof dressing and gloves worn wherever there is contact with blood.

People with HIV who are living independently and working should be encouraged to continue doing so. Some changes may be needed to make life more manageable, but do not be overprotective. Everyone must find their own way of living with the virus. Be available. Show you care.

Once someone has been diagnosed as having HIV, there are some very important decisions to be made. For instance, who should be told? Most people agree that it is wisest to tell as few people as possible, but again, this is up to the individual. Serious consequences for employment, housing, insurance and other important parts of life can result from breaches of confidentiality.

No one knows what the future holds for us. People with HIV or AIDS know that their future is more uncertain, so today becomes more important. I am grateful to Dublin AIDS Alliance for their help in putting together the following thoughts and suggestions that may help you:

Don't avoid your friend or child. Be the friend or parent you have always been.

Always phone before visiting to make sure it's okay. Let your friend make the decision – they may not feel up to visitors that day. Don't be offended if that's the case – offer to phone again.

Call and offer to bring a special meal. Share the washing-up.

Gauge the length of your stay and don't overstay your welcome.

Go for walks or outings together but if your friend is ill, be aware of their limitations.

If your friend or child has children of their own, help to look after them.

Don't be afraid to ask about the illness. People need to talk.

Remember that everyone has good days and bad days. On bad days, treat people with extra care and compassion.

Tell the person how good they look, but only if it's realistic. If their appearance has changed, don't ignore it. Be gentle, but never lie.

Know your own limitations, and don't feel guilty if you have to say no. You will be of no use if you wear yourself out.

Ask how the person is coping financially.

Illness can bring a great loss of control over life, but try not to make decisions for other people.

Be prepared if your friend gets angry at you for no obvious reason. Anger and frustration are often taken out on those people who are most loved.

People with AIDS get opportunistic infections, but they do recover from these, so send get-well cards.

If you share a religion, try praying together.

Remember that illness does not make people instantly lovable or right in everything they say. If you disagree with them, say so. Don't patronise or humour them.

Bring a positive attitude. It's catching.

Talk about the future. Remember that people with AIDS do have a future – albeit a little more uncertain than most.

DOES ONE LESBIAN PLAY AT BEING THE MAN AND THE OTHER THE WOMAN?

In most relationships one partner is usually more dominant than the other. This has very little to do with traditional gender roles, because women are very often the dominant partner. Within any relationship a couple will determine the ground rules and operate according to each person's strengths and weaknesses. Thankfully the day is largely gone when men and women stuck to rigidly defined roles, and there is generally much more equality in relationships now.

This question is most often asked in relation to sexual practices, however, and in order to answer this question I spoke to a lesbian from Lesbians Organising Together, Dublin:

'I am in a long-term relationship, and I find this question amusing. Our relationship is based on equality. We have never really discussed our roles within the relationship. We found that we each automatically took care of certain things. We both work, but I only work part-time, so for practical reasons I do most of the housework. We try and discuss any issues as they arise, so everything is done in an organised and friendly manner. I'd say most relationships operate this way though.

'When it comes to our sexual relationship, there is complete equality. One is not more powerful than the other. There are no demands. Sex should always be a mutual thing, and that is the way it is with us. We don't think in terms of male and female roles – we are both lesbians and we make love in our own way and I don't think that this should be discussed anyway. I don't ask heterosexuals what they do in bed, nor does it interest me. We are happy as a couple, and I think that's as much as anybody needs to know.

'It strikes me that this kind of question would be asked by a man, who feels that women could not do without him and especially when thinking about sexual intercourse. Many such men find it incomprehensible to think that another woman could take his place, and be a fulfilling partner at the same time and it must be said that this is a constant source of amusement to gay women.'

ARE GAY MEN EFFEMINATE?

There is a common stereotype of the homosexual as an effeminate, weak man, who wears flamboyant clothes, has a limp wrist and is interested in interior design and artistic matters. However, the vast majority of gay men look, act and speak just like heterosexual men and in fact are different from heterosexuals only in so far as they are attracted to men. It is true to say that within the gay community there is far less pressure on men to conform to the macho stereotypes of the straight world, so that perhaps there is a greater freedom to indulge in interests which may be shared by straight men but not practised because the straight world puts enormous pressure on people to act like 'real' men. The 'typical' straight man – football-loving, beer-drinking, who doesn't help with the housework and the kids – is also a stereotype. The truth is that all men, gay or straight, fall somewhere between the two.

DO GAY MEN WEAR WOMEN'S CLOTHES?

It is a common myth that gay men dress up in women's clothes. However, transvestites – men who wear women's clothes for pleasure – are almost inevitably heterosexual: it is the knowledge that under the female apparel there is a male body that is important to them, and many transvestites are happily married, with understanding wives. Occasionally at parties gay men do dress up in women's clothing. This is known as drag, and is very different from transvestisism: it's always very over-the-top and a deliberate parody, and is usually meant as a celebration of difference. It is never done for sexual pleasure.

Neither do gay men feel that they are women in men's bodies. Transsexuals – those who have operations to 'become' one of the opposite sex (and this happens as frequently with women as it does with men) – are not gay. They genuinely feel that they are trapped in the wrong body, and a transsexual man wants only to become a woman. Transsexual men may sleep with members of their own sex, but they do it because they feel that they are really women in men's bodies. Lesbians and gay men are perfectly happy being the sex they are. Transsexuality is concerned with the gender one feels oneself to *be;* homosexuality is to do with the gender one is attracted *to*.

MY CHILD OR FRIEND HAS COME OUT TO ME. I'M STILL A LITTLE CONFUSED. WHAT DO I DO NOW?

If someone close has just come out to you, you are probably feeling shocked and surprised. This is perfectly fine. If you are a parent, it can be very difficult to realise that many of your hopes and dreams for your child – the 'traditional' marriage, perhaps, and children – will probably not now come to pass. You may have strong religious feelings against homosexuality and be finding it difficult to face the fact that your son or daughter is going against so many of your beliefs. Many people feel guilty and that perhaps it is their fault that their child is gay – but remember, this is not the case. And many feel embarrassed and ashamed, and wonder what neighbours and relatives might think.

Firstly, take the time to think through your initial reaction. The fact that you are reading this book means that you are willing to take a very positive step. Don't lose your temper – remember, your child is an adult now. If you feel you need some time, say so.

This is a time when it can often be very useful to talk to a third party. Many parents have been helped through this time of initial shock by Parents Enquiry, a special helpline set up specifically to help parents through this difficult time. There is a list of helplines and contacts at the back of this book that you may find useful.

Above all, at this stage remember that someone's homosexuality is only a very small part of their personality. She or he is still the same person that they always were. It may take time for a parent to accept this fact, but it is better, and certainly wiser, to sit down and talk. Try to hear what they are saying, not what you think they are saying. You may not approve of their choices, their lifestyle or their friends, but that's okay. Your child or friend may not approve of your choices or lifestyle either. You are dealing with an adult now, and the two of you will have to come to accept each other on equal terms.

If you do disagree with homosexuality, try to accept the gay person for herself or himself. Remember that homosexuality is just an aspect of their personality. Don't pass on the opportunity to show love and friendship to this person, because that is all they are

49

asking of you.

If your child has been abandoned to loneliness, try to find it in your heart to reach out to them. Whether they are fourteen or forty, they need to know that they have a family who cares for them. Relationships can be just as difficult for gay people as they are for straight people. If you are a parent, try to discuss this area with your child in order to put your fears to rest. Try to support your child in relationships. Don't close off such an important part of their life. Don't be afraid to mention their partner's name, and to enquire about them. If your child's relationship does break up, try your best to be supportive. They will be hurting and just to know that you care will be a great help.

Remember, you don't love and befriend heterosexuals because of their sexuality, but because of their lovable characteristics. Don't reject someone because of their sexuality.

TURNING THE TABLES

Gay people are often asked strange questions. Often this is because their interrogators have a strictly heterosexual view of what is 'normal', and perceive gay people's sexuality as more than just a part of their lives. Sexuality is just one part of heterosexual's lives, too, and heterosexuals do not see themselves only in terms of their sexuality. What would it be like if the tables were turned?

1. What is the cause of your heterosexuality?
2. When did you first realise you might be heterosexual?
3. Have you told your parents?
4. What did your parents think of it?
5. Are there others like you in your family?

6. Would you say that you had an inadequate mother or father?
7. Don't you think your heterosexuality might be a phase you are going through?
8. Isn't it possible that what really you need is a good same-sex lover?
9. What do you actually do in bed?
10. Why are there so few stable relationships amongst heterosexuals?
11. Is it because heterosexuals are so promiscuous?
12. There seem to be very few happy heterosexuals – have you considered aversion therapy?
13. More than 90 per cent of child molesters are thought to be heterosexuals. Would you feel comfortable about entrusting your children's education to heterosexual teachers?

Instead, relax and be lighthearted:
1. Do not run screaming from the room. This is rude!
2. If you must back away, do so slowly and with discretion.
3. Do not assume that they are attracted to you.
4. Do not assume that they are not attracted to you.
5. Do not assume that you are not attracted to them.
6. Do not think that they are as interested in meeting a heterosexual as you are in meeting a homosexual.
7. Do not immediately start talking about your boyfriend or girlfriend in order to make it clear that you are straight.
8. Do not ask them how they got that way.
9. Do not assume that they are dying to talk about being gay.
10. Do not expect them to refrain from saying anything about being gay.

CONCLUSION

In Ireland, though not in Britain, it is already illegal, to discriminate against lesbians and gay men in the workplace, and although discrimination has not ended, gay people at least have the law on their side. The day is, thankfully, gone now when gay people lived in fear of being discovered. However, there is much yet to be done: while gay men and lesbians are no longer treated as criminals, they are discriminated against in areas such as education, the provision of goods and services, and access to accommodation. Amnesty International recently stated that 'protecting the human rights of gays and lesbians is an international responsibility and is a struggle to be waged by all people, just as the struggle for human rights for women, for the disappeared, and for the survivors of torture is an international responsibility and is waged by all people... Homosexuals in many parts of the world live in constant fear of government persecution – afraid that their private acts of love and public acts of courage will be punished by governments in secret torture chambers, at clandestine "safe houses" and on midnight raids'.

We each need to remember that we have been brought up in a predominantly heterosexual society. This does not mean, however, that heterosexuality is the only way of living. Our more multi-racial, multi-cultural and cosmopolitan society has shown us that difference is a positive thing, whether it is difference of colour, religion, politics, language or sexuality. The more we accept this, the better our society is for all its members.

PART 2

True-Life Stories

JIM EGAN

I am the father of a gay son, and I am also a member of Parents Enquiry, which is a support group for the parents of gay children. We are not counsellors – we are parents who can share with others from our own experience. Often this can be the most helpful and welcome source for a parent, to help them to deal with the initial shock they will experience when their child comes out to them. Parents usually have questions which they want answered, and they want to discuss any worries or concerns they may have.

My own son is gay. When he was doing his Leaving Cert. he went through a very hard time. To be honest, he was on the verge of a nervous breakdown, and he was taken into hospital for treatment.

I realised that he was under a lot of pressure to do well in his exams at school. The final year of school is always a very difficult time for any young person. This was a particularly worrying time for me though, especially since my wife had died some years previous to this.

I visited my son in hospital every day, and tried to encourage him to get well again. I knew that his school exams were of no importance at a time like this. It was so sad to see him lying there, and he was so obviously troubled.

It was during his stay in hospital that my son first came out. Of course, I was so concerned about getting him well that I didn't really think about what my son was saying to me.

It was a short while later that I began to think about the implications of my son being gay, and I decided to find out more about the whole subject. I contacted the Gay Switchboard, and they put me in touch with Parents Enquiry. I felt that I needed to talk about my child to someone who would understand. I think that parents need to talk things over and share their feelings with another person, outside of family and friends.

My son has been in a relationship for two years now. His partner is welcome in my home, as are any of his other gay or lesbian friends. He has also come out to his friends at college, and has met with complete acceptance there. Also, some of our neighbours know that he is gay and they don't have a problem with it. My son attends meetings of Reach, a gay Christian group. I think that this is a good thing, and I attended a very lovely carol service there last Christmas.

Before all this happened with my son, I had no idea that there were so many gay people. I have attended various functions with my son, and I have had the pleasure of meeting many very nice people. It was difficult for me the first time I saw gay people dancing together at a function – but from their viewpoint, this was a safe place to be.

I myself have just started as a volunteer with AIDS Alliance. I feel that AIDS is a very lonely illness. When I was younger, cancer was the illness which was unspoken. It was a stigma. I think that we need to remember back to these times, when people used to be afraid of cancer as they are now afraid of AIDS.

There are many hopes dashed when a person comes out to their parents. There will never be a marriage ceremony, nor will there be grandchildren. These are very difficult things for a parent to accept. However, any child will bring their own joys to the parent regardless of these things.

I would advise any parent that if their child comes out to them, say nothing – don't say a word. Instead, try to relax, and not fly off the handle. Take time to think things over, and then talk about it a few days or weeks later. Life is very short, and we need to try to make the best of it. Your child is the same person they have always been. They are not going to change. They are still your son or your daughter, and they still need your love. All your child wants is to be loved and accepted.

LISA

A friend of mine came out to me recently. We met at a yoga class about a year ago. We seemed to get on really well from the start. Sometimes people just seem to click, and that's how it was with us.

One day in conversation she said that she was feeling very angry, that people at work had been saying things which she didn't agree with. She seemed to be very upset about it, so I asked her what was it that had made her angry. She told me that some people in work had been making comments about gay people, saying how they were only interested in sex, and how it was a disgusting way to live. She then told me that the reason that she was so angry was because she is a lesbian herself.

I felt dumbfounded. I wasn't expecting her to say anything like that to me.

She asked me how I felt about her being gay, and I said that I felt okay. I said that I didn't have a problem with gay people. However, I was dishonest. It was what I wanted to say from my head, but it wasn't what I was feeling inside. I had always believed that we are all free to be individuals and to express ourselves, and I was very surprised to find that I reacted differently when I was actually faced with a gay person.

Then I started to worry in case I'd been sending out any signals to her. Did she think that I was gay too? Was this her reason for telling me about herself? All sorts of thoughts raced around my head. It was a very confusing time for me.

I decided not to see my friend for a while. I needed some time to sort out my thinking and feelings. I was concerned to get the message across to my friend that I was not gay. I was not in a relationship with a man, but I was still heterosexual. At the same time I wanted her to know that I wanted her friendship. I wanted her to know that I wasn't rejecting her in any way. I felt quite certain about my own sexuality, and I wanted my friend to be assured of this.

My friend is in a relationship, but I find it very difficult to ask her anything about this. I feel that it is intrusive. But then if I don't ask her about her partner, I feel that I'm not acknowledging her gay lifestyle. This whole area is very difficult for me to deal with at the moment.

Nowadays, I still see my friend quite regularly. I do value her friendship very much. I know that she hasn't come out to her parents. She feels that they would reject her. She has said that she has heard them making comments about gay people on television, and she definitely won't say anything about herself now.

I still have questions about gay people myself. I would like to know for example, whether one partner is more dominant than the other. I'd like to know how gay people meet. My friend says that she has never been on the gay scene. So how can she meet other gay people? Maybe these are things that I can come to discuss with her in time. In the meantime I would just like to enjoy her friendship.

BARRY

I am twenty-seven years old and come from Galway. I've known I was gay from a very young age: I have memories of being attracted to men since I was about seven years old – later on I was attracted to girls for a year or so, but by the time I was thirteen I was certain of my sexuality. I kept it very much to myself – I grew up hearing negative comments about gays and even joined in them myself – until I was eighteen, when I came out to a group of friends in college, a couple of whom were gay themselves. I never made a conscious decision to come out – I just said it at the spur of the moment.

I'm out to one brother, and to my friends, but I am no longer on a crusade about it. If most people asked, I'd say yes. I think my mother knows, but there is a world of difference between knowing and being told. In Ireland more than most countries, there has been an enormous cultural change between generations. I don't want to tell my parents anything that would hurt them. I also think she'd worry about AIDS. Of course it"s an extremely important issue and as a gay man I know I am at risk, but I think it's important to separate the issues of being gay and having AIDS. I'm a gay man, and every time I see a programme about gays it talks about AIDS, and the fact is that the vast majority of the people I know do *not* have AIDS or HIV. In fact after living in London three years, the first person I knew with the disease was in Galway.

After college I moved to London. The city is a magnet to gay people and I found it very appealing, and very liberating. However, I now think that I would prefer to live in Ireland. Despite many preconceptions, I feel that Ireland is far more tolerant. Pre-reform Ireland had inherited repugnant anti-homosexual legislation, but on the whole, as far as I am aware, this was largely ignored, and there was very little prosecution. In Britain, on the other hand, it is commonly thought that the legislation is, or was, more liberal. In fact the practical meaning of the legislation is that there are *exceptions* under which homosexuality is legal. Also, people in Britain are generally unaware that there are a great many gay men in prison for homosexual practices. I feel this is because Britain considers itself a democracy but actually lacks any tradition of human rights, just as it lacks a written constitution and bill of rights. Post-reform Ireland is much more exciting – not just because of the laws relating to homosexuality but also because of the laws protecting people under the Incitement to Hatred Act. In London I am perfectly free to fire someone for being gay – thankfully, that's not the case here.

I think that this Irish tolerance is linked to Catholicism. Non-Catholic countries find it harder to separate the public from the private. Catholicism gives us a marker but, providing something isn't shoved in our faces, we have an unspoken cultural accommodation of anyone who misses this mark – for instance those involved in broken marriages, adultery, homosexuality. It's something that's often found in Mediterranean countries. I don't find this dishonest but liberating. I would describe myself ethnically as Catholic, though a secular Catholic – informed Catholic values have given a great cultural richness to my life. Catholicism doesn't oppress me – oppression is internal. This became very important and very clear to me when I was in New York at a time when the anti-discrimination activities of groups such as Act Up and OutRage! manifested themselves as an uninformed anti-Catholicism – members would disrupt Mass at St Patrick's Cathedral every Sunday. I found myself being forced to choose between my identity as a gay man, and my identity as a Catholic Irish man, and I chose to be seen as Irish. I find gay political dogma worse than Catholic dogma, because it is unquestionable.

I've had one serious relationship, in London. It lasted three years and at the time I thought it would be permanent. However, Deepak was very involved with his family, who didn't know he was gay, and I think that in a gay relationship that makes commitment more difficult. It's easier when you're abroad. Now I'm not sure if I want another relationship. There are enormous advantages to being a single man, gay or straight. Because I earn enough to be comfortable, because I don't have a biological clock ticking, and because I can have sex whenever I want, there is no *need* for me to commit to someone, in the way that straight people, particularly straight women, need to. I don't rule it out, and my relationship with Deepak was, and is, very important to me, but I feel that in the absence of children, short-term relationships are just as valid as permanent commitments. Straight people don't do all that well in their relationships either. The advantage of being gay is that there can be a great deal more personal freedom – no staying together for the sake of the children. I'd like to meet someone, more for companionship than anything, but I wouldn't stay in anything second-rate.

I'd like to live in Ireland again. I've lived in England a long time, and have developed an identity there as a gay man, and as an Irish man. It's very attractive to form these allegiances when you're younger. B : now I don't need the feeling of belonging that this brings, and I want to live as an individual.

FRANK
My ex-wife is a lesbian. We were married for twelve years, and we have two children.

I met Caroline at a party when we were both 21. We

hit it off straight away, and we started going out together.

After a whirlwind romance, we decided to get married. We both wanted the big, traditional wedding, and so that's the way we did it. There was no expense spared. It was a wonderful day, and all our family and friends enjoyed it very much. We went to Paris for our honeymoon, and we had the most marvellous time. We were both virgins and so we were completely naive about sex, but we just experimented, and everything seemed to be fine.

We set up home in a small rural town. I worked in the bank, and I had to spend a lot of time flying back and forward to various international branches, so I was away from home a lot. However, Caroline was always a very independent person, and she was contented enough staying at home and keeping things going there. She always had friends and never seemed to be lonely. Two years into the marriage we started a family. Our first child was a daughter, and we were both very happy with life, or so I thought.

I later discovered that when our daughter was nearly two years old, my wife became involved with another woman, a friend who lived nearby. She was single, and a lesbian. I don't really know how things started, or who started the affair. I knew that they were very friendly, but I didn't know that things had gone any further than that, until one weekend I returned from London and she sat me down and told me what was going on.

I couldn't believe what she was saying. It would have been bad enough if she had told me that she was having an affair with another man, but to be seeing another woman was too much for me to take in.

We argued about it for a few weeks. I was so hurt, but I didn't want to lose her. I tried to talk to her and to persuade her not to walk away from the marriage. I told her that I would try not to be away from home so much. She agreed to stay with me, but she did not agree to stop seeing her friend.

Over the following months I tried very hard to make things right between us. I tried to be a good husband, and to be a good lover. Caroline became pregnant with our second child. Again we were both really pleased. However, I knew we could never go back to the way we were. Our second daughter was born. We had a very comfortable lifestyle and to the outside world we were the happiest couple around. But this was so far from the truth.

I think that Caroline went through a very difficult time after the birth of our second child. She didn't seem to know who she was, and I think that she felt that she actually loved two people. Things could not continue as they were, and we both knew this. Caroline said that she wanted to live with her friend, and that's what she did.

She is still living with her today, and she has the two children as well. I see my children very regularly. I'm not in favour of her having the children, but with my work I know that I could not bring them up on my own.

I'm still very hurt at what has happened. I don't hold it against Caroline, because it could have been the other way around. I think that you have to make the best of situations. I don't blame Caroline's friend either. She is a very nice woman, and she has her own business, so my children still have a good lifestyle.

I know that there must be other men who are in my situation. I have never actually met any, but I know that I'm not the only one that this has happened to.

Caroline and I are divorced now. I have gone out with other women, but only for one-night stands. I think that sometimes I need to prove to myself that I can still be attractive to women as a man.

I have nothing against any gay or lesbian person. I think that people are born that way. Maybe society makes it very difficult for gay people to be themselves, and they feel they have to marry. It certainly shouldn't be that way, though.

PHILIPPA

I have known my friend Mary for many years. We met when we were in our late teens through a mutual friend. We have seen our friendship grow over the years, and we have seen each other through many ups and downs. We share a lot of common interests and we both have the same slightly crazy sense of humour.

I would never have guessed that Mary was gay. We used to go out to nightclubs together with guys. Mary was quite popular with the guys, and would go out with them for a drink. She was nearly engaged to a guy years ago. He really loved her, but one day she wrote him a letter and she told him that she couldn't stay in a relationship with him any longer. She didn't give him any explanation, and the guy was completely devastated. Looking back now, she probably did him a favour. She must have known that she was gay, and probably knew it would be unfair to the guy to marry him.

We don't really discuss things like that together. We never interfere in each other's lives, and that is probably why our friendship has lasted for so many years.

I remember the day that Mary told me she was gay. She phoned me and asked me if I would meet her in a hotel in town for a drink. I had been thinking to myself that she had been working up to telling me something for a few weeks previous to this. I had wondered what she was going to tell me. I had suspected that she was going to tell me that she was either gay or pregnant! I knew that her news was something big, and I prepared myself to hear either of these two things.

When she finally told me, I sort of dismissed the whole thing, and laughed it off. We sat and had a few drinks, and chatted the day away. She had been terrified that I would walk away from her, and not want to know her any more. I am sorry that she ever thought that in the first place. I would never walk away from our friendship. She has been such a good friend to me, and has stood by me when things were bad in my life, and so I hope that I would always be there for her.

I think that I was a bit shocked when she told me that she was gay, because for quite a few weeks later I couldn't talk about it. I have strong religious beliefs and my religion teaches that being gay is wrong. Mary was the first gay person I had ever personally known, and so I needed time to think about things.

Now I try to see Mary as the same friend I have always had, and to keep my religious beliefs separate. I don't believe that a gay person will go to hell or anything like that. It's just that I've been brought up to believe that homosexuality is a deviant behaviour.

I have never really spoken to Mary about what being gay means to her or how she lives her life. I don't want to pry into her private life. I know that she doesn't go to gay bars much because she still prefers to go out with the same crowd of friends that we've always had. Everybody on the circle now knows that Mary is gay, and it's never been a problem.

I know that Mary has been going out with another woman for a while now. I feel a bit awkward about this. I've only met this woman a few times, and she seems nice enough, but I didn't know what to say the first time I met her. However, I feel that I may get to know Mary's friend as a person, and I will then stop thinking of her as being just a lesbian. I know that probably sounds prejudiced, but it's not meant to be.

DAVID

I am thirty-two years old, and I am a gay man. I am happy to be gay. It's not something that I feel ashamed about. I'm a fairly happy-go-lucky kind of person. I enjoy my life on the whole, except that I can feel lonely at times.

When I was a child, I was bullied at school, and called all sorts of names. I don't really know why – maybe because I wasn't a sporty person. Sometimes, that's all it takes for a child to be picked from the crowd. This bullying went on for some time, and after a while my parents brought me to a child psychiatrist. I have no idea why they did this – maybe it was an attempt to make me into a macho little boy. It only made me feel more different, now that I was going to see a shrink – word gets around the classroom very quickly. When I was slightly older, I was sent to see a different psychiatrist. This one wanted to put me on tablets which would deaden my sexual drive. I was a bit young to have a sex drive in the first place.

I think that my parents knew that I was gay, and they wanted to make sure that I never started to practise gay sex. I refused to be put on any such medication. I knew that I was attracted to men and not women, and I didn't have a problem with that. Why should I be put on medication? I don't believe that I'm gay because of anything that happened in my childhood. I believe that I was born gay.

I have now been working in the gay community for five years. I help to put together a monthly gay newspaper. I like working there – most of the time. At times it gets very busy, and you'd just like to walk out and go and have a coffee somewhere. But every job is like that.

My parents won't discuss my work. They can't even mention the name of the place, and they never ask me when I come home at night how my day has been, or if I had a good day at work. My parents never want to know if I'm meeting another man for a drink. However, I work with women too, and if I tell them that I'm meeting a woman for a drink after work, they want to know all the details. They are always interested in me meeting a nice girl, and they want to know all about any girl I ever mention to them. The funny thing is that nearly all the women I know are gay. My parents just won't accept that I'm not going to marry someone and settle down.

I do find that being a gay man is a very lonely life. Also, I have to be on my guard all the time. You have to learn to protect yourself, and be wary of people. Sometimes gay people are beaten up. Some people have been attacked walking out of a gay bar. It doesn't happen very often, but it does happen.

I think that when I decided to come out and live as a gay man, I was deciding to live my life alone. I don't want sex just for the sake of it. I would like to have a relationship. I do have friends, but I am often lonely. It would be nice to have someone special in my life, though I think that there are many more pressures on gay couples than there on heterosexual couples. It is exactly the pressure of trying to live as a gay couple, which often helps to break a relationship.

I don't think that it's ever the fault of parents if their child is gay. Parents can have many problems with children, but I think that if a person is basically happy, then parents should be happy enough too. Many parents have to live with the fact that their child is a drug addict, for example. I think that parents with a gay child need to ask themselves, do I want my child to be in my life? If the answer to this question is yes, then the parents have to learn to treat their child as an adult, and let them be themselves. It's a great pity for a parent to lose a relationship with their child just because the child is gay. Life is too short for such sadness. Parents will never always approve of their child's behaviour or thinking, but that should not be a reason for rejection.

ANN-MARIE

My sister is a lesbian. It doesn't really bother me in the least. We grew up in a quiet suburb in a fairly large town. Growing up in our family was a happy experience. Our parents gave us a very secure upbringing, and we were quite a close family.

My sister was never really different from anybody else. She was good at school – very studious – and she was always out with friends having a good time. She was a member of more groups and she did more courses than I care to remember. I remember that she had a string of boyfriends when she was a teenager. She knew how to enjoy herself, and I always looked up to her when I was younger.

My sister first told me she was gay two years ago when we were on holiday together. I had been wondering about her for a short while before that. I had decided not to say anything about it to her, and if she was gay she could tell me in her own time.

When I initially heard that she was gay, I felt a little bit shocked, but I think that's quite a natural reaction. I decided that we were on holiday, so there was no point in spoiling the rest of it. We actually had a great time afterwards, because now it was out in the open, and we could both relax and enjoy ourselves.

I don't think that gay people are any different from anybody else. It's nobody's business what you do in bed, or who with – as long as it's legal. I think that it's okay to be gay, provided that you keep it a private affair. I feel a bit uncomfortable seeing gay people in public, and I don't agree with gay people parading through the streets. I don't think it's necessary to proclaim your gayness to the world.

I'm glad that my sister told me that she is gay, because I feel that I know a bit more about her life now. She lives with another woman, and they both seem to be very happy together. They are a really good couple and are best friends. I like that, although I must admit I feel a bit intrusive in their company. I try to talk to them both as people, and we do have a good laugh together sometimes.

None of my own friends have said anything negative about my sister. They think like me that it is a private matter. We are all in our mid-twenties, though, so I suppose we are much more accepting than perhaps older generations would be.

My sister hasn't told my parents that she is gay. She says that she is not sure how they will take it, and she is afraid that they would take it badly. My mother has been trying to work out the situation for herself, and has been watching various programmes on the TV about gay people. I think that my mother would like to ask my sister about being gay, and maybe one day she will ask her out straight. My dad never mentions anything. He has his own business and he keeps himself busy at work. He is close to my sister and I know that they talk together quite a bit, but usually about work. They are both workaholics.

I just want my sister to be happy. I am proud of her for who she is. She is successful in her own life, and I hope that both she and her partner will always be happy.

I have met some of my sister's friends, and they are all very nice, ordinary people. I have been to a gay bar with them, and I actually enjoyed it. It was a relaxing atmosphere, and they had much more to talk about

71

than sex! Sometimes people have all kinds of weird ideas about gay people, and their lifestyle, but I think that if people took the time to find out more about gay people, they would find that they are just ordinary people, living ordinary lives. I don't want to stand on a platform for gay people, because there are other people in society who have to live with prejudice as well, and who have also been marginalised – for example disabled people. I hope that prejudice in society will diminish for all people, including gay people.

MARIE

I am the mother of a lesbian. My daughter hasn't told me that she is gay, but I have put things together for myself over the years, and she is now living with a woman.

Lesbian and gay matters were never discussed when I was growing up. I'm in my mid-fifties now. Sometimes there would be a bit of gossip about someone being different, but it just wasn't discussed – nothing to do with sex was discussed really.

My daughter was my first child, and she was very spoiled. Patricia was always a very outgoing girl. She enjoyed all kinds of interests – swimming, hockey, dancing, reading, and she loved all kinds of music. Basically, she just loved life, and she still does. She was good at her school work, and she went on to college to study to be a social worker. She is a very caring person, and always had a good way with people. She would get a bit too involved with people's problems, I felt, but I think that was only her enthusiasm.

Patricia was always daddy's girl. We used to go on

shopping sprees from time to time, and buy new clothes. She was never a follower of fashion though – it was always jeans and shirts. Her two younger sisters are the complete opposite.

Patricia always had lots of friends around the house, both male and female. They used to come over and just sit and chat, and listen to music. They were all young and carefree, and I used to enjoy hearing the laughter in the house. She started going out with boys when she was fourteen. She usually stayed with them for a couple of years, then it would all end. When she was in her mid-teens, it was the time of punk rock, and we were dreading any kind of problem with her dyeing her hair or drinking or coming home with safety pins in her ears. Thankfully, Patricia was never involved in any of that kind of behaviour. She never smoked, and I don't think that she ever drank until she was at least twenty.

Patricia was always a very level-headed person. She moved away from home when she finished college. She wanted to move to Dublin, to the city. We live in a large town in Ireland, but she didn't want to stay there. Before she left home, she was going out with a boy from the town. They had been together for about two years. I knew though that she didn't have strong feelings for him, but he was crazy about her. All of a sudden, things were over between them, and she was moving to Dublin. I never asked her what went wrong. It was her decision, and that was that.

Patricia was always a lucky girl, and when she moved to Dublin, she found a job very quickly. She found herself a flat, and started to make new friends.

She had a good friend, Geraldine, who she used to

bring home with her at weekends. They were very close, and they seemed to get on well together. I never thought a thing about it, but after a while I started to sense that there was more to this relationship than just a friendship. They would look at each other in a certain way, and I could sense that they were gay.

I didn't really allow myself to think about it very much. I didn't want to ask any questions, and I was quite ignorant on the whole subject really. I started to read articles in magazines about lesbians, and watch Oprah Winfrey shows on the subject, so that I could learn more. I didn't know who to ask about it, and I didn't really want to discuss the subject anyway.

Today, my daughter is thirty-five and she shares a house with another woman, who is a bit older than her. She still hasn't told me that she's gay, but I don't mind too much. I've tried to bring the subject out into the open, but I find it very difficult to be direct about it. I feel that this is a part of my daughter's life that I'll never share.

I always try to let my daughter know that I love her, and that I'm proud of her. I feel that she has always tried to protect the family by not telling us about that part of her life. She may also be afraid to mention the subject of homosexuality to her father, because he would have very traditional views about things. He loves her very much though, and nothing would stop him from loving her. We would never feel ashamed of Patricia.

I think that people must be born gay. I feel sorry that gay people have to live with so much secrecy. To be happy in life, and enjoy good health are what counts. I wish these things for all my children.

ROBERT

I am in my early thirties, and I work for a Christian organisation. I would describe myself as a gay man, although I don't practise homosexuality.

In my present job I work with young people. I don't feel that I'm endangering anybody. I'm certainly not out to seduce anybody, and I tend not to mention anything about being gay at work.

I believe that the Christian Church needs to widen its arms to reach out to gay people, with compassion and understanding. It's not helpful to anyone to condemn gay people. There are a few Christian groups nowadays though who realise that, and who are trying to reach out to gay people and accept and understand them.

I find it difficult to define myself as gay, because the media have provided society with such a negative image of homosexuality, and also because I come from a Catholic background, where it is taught that homosexuality is wrong. I don't want to be associated with the popular media images of gay people. I am not sex-mad. I am not suffering from some kind of illness, and I am not trying to seduce young people into a gay lifestyle. This kind of imagery makes it very difficult for me to label myself as being gay. It certainly doesn't instil confidence in me to come out to people. I actually told my mother about my gayness in a letter. I thought that I could express myself better in written form, than make some fumbling attempt at talking to her face to face. She was very good about the whole thing, and said that she wished that I had talked to her sooner. I felt glad that she knew now, and I'm pleased that she accepts me. I came out to my brother and sister and they were okay too. They weren't overjoyed by my news, but they did accept me.

I don't really know what kind of a reaction a person can expect when you come out to someone. Rejection is what you would fear most. I know that it must come as a shock at first, but unless people are completely homophobic, I don't think that there should be any huge problems.

The Bible says that we can all be accepted by God, because we have all sinned, and God loves sinners. He knows that we are nothing without Him, but he treats us all equally, whoever we are, and wherever we're coming from. God wants to meet our needs. I know that my desire to be loved and affirmed can be met in God. I think that is what we all look for in life – to be loved and affirmed.

I am happy with my life as it stands at the moment. I don't know what the future holds for me – maybe celibacy, maybe even marriage. I would like to see a place in Ireland where gay people could meet and talk about their beliefs and their hopes and wishes. I would like to see the Church involved in such a group, because we all have things to learn.

MARGARET

I am now thirty-six years old, and I live in a small town. I was married for six years to a gay man.

I grew up in a small town in Ireland, and I went out with a few boys before I met Jonathan. We got on really well, and within two years of meeting we were married. We had a lot of friends. We both worked, and generally we had a good life.

We bought a lovely house, and we put a lot of time and money into making it our dream home. We even shared the gardening, which neither of us was good at, but we wanted to make things as comfortable as we could. We'd have friends around for dinner, and go away on foreign holidays. We had a good lifestyle by all accounts.

One day we were out for dinner, just the two of us, and in the middle of the conversation, he suddenly asked me what would I think if he had had a gay relationship. I just laughed it off, and said something about the fact that we all have a past. I never gave it a second thought. We finished our meal, and then went off to a nightclub. Life went on as normal.

After a few months, Jonathan started drinking heavily. He would come home from work, and start to drink before dinner. When we were out with friends, he would drink twice as much as anybody else. Life suddenly became very unhappy. He wouldn't discuss anything with me. He began to realise himself that he was drinking too much, but he wouldn't do anything about it.

My own self-esteem started to go down. I was left playing second fiddle to a bottle of whisky. I was embarrassed to go out with any of our friends. I couldn't concentrate at work. I felt stressed out all the time, and I felt too ashamed to talk about it to anyone.

One day, Jonathan came home from work, and said that he was going to see a counsellor about his drinking problems, and that he would start to go to Alcoholics Anonymous. He had been talking to a welfare officer in work, and had decided that it was time to do something about it. He continued to go to therapy for some months, and things improved quite a bit. But I felt very nervous about our marriage. I wondered if things would ever get back to the way they used to be.

However, the worst was yet to come. One night, Jonathan came home from his therapy session, and said that he had something to tell me. He told me that he was living a lie, and that he was gay. He said that he had never been unfaithful to me, but he knew that he was sexually attracted to men, and not women. He said that he couldn't pretend any more. He didn't want us to continue our marriage under false pretences.

I was completely flabbergasted. I didn't know what to say or do. I felt angry at him for deceiving me. I felt hurt and rejected. It was the worst time of my life. Suddenly my whole identity was gone. I didn't know what my life was about any more. I couldn't concentrate in work, and I ended up going to see a counsellor myself. I couldn't understand how he could have hurt me so much, and bring such unhappiness to me.

Jonathan moved out of our house a few weeks later. We couldn't discuss anything. I was devastated. I had to tell my family and friends that Jonathan had left me, but I couldn't tell them why. I really didn't want to talk to anybody about my failed marriage.

One day I received a letter from Jonathan telling me that he had found a new job in England, and asking me if I would have dinner with him before he left.

I was actually glad to hear from him. We met for dinner and we talked all night long. There was so much to talk about, and although our marriage was over, we had been good friends too. I think that night we managed to salvage our friendship.

I sometimes write to Jonathan today, and he writes to me. I never ask him about his gay life. I don't know if he is in a gay relationship.

For myself, I haven't been out with another man since Jonathan left me. I don't want to even think about another relationship at the moment.

I have nothing against gay people. I know a few gay people at work, and I've always had a good friendship with them. But I wouldn't like anyone to go through a false marriage like I did. I know that it must be difficult for gay people to come out, and to be accepted by society. I don't think that they should marry, though, and hope that their homosexuality will go away.

I'm still going to counselling, and I am looking forward to the day when I can truly start my life afresh. Maybe I will be lucky enough to find a second relationship. I'd like to think that we all deserve a second chance – and I wish that for Jonathan too.

ANTHONY

My friend Mick is gay, and I think that he needs to have his head examined. He has lost a lot of friends since he told us that he was gay. I still talk to him, but I don't tell the rest of my friends that, or they would start to call me a queer as well.

Mick and I grew up together. We live in a large corporation estate, and it is definitely not acceptable to be gay. If people in our area knew that a person was gay they'd put his windows in – and it has happened. There was a lesbian living down the road from our house, and word spread around that she was living with another woman. She had some kids, because she used to be married, and I heard that they were bullied in school, and they had to move away from the area.

Nobody has given Mick a bad time, because nobody really knows much about him. The friends that he told wouldn't do anything to hurt him, but they just don't talk to him now, or only in passing. Maybe it's because nobody knows much about gay people around here. Here, if anybody is seen to be different in any way, they become an easy target. For instance, we have some Mormons living near us, and they get an awful time of it.

Mick's own family threw him out of the house when he told them he was gay. They said that they had disowned him, that no son of theirs was going to live as a queer. They told him never to come near the house again, because they didn't want the neighbours talking about him. I think they told everyone that he had moved to England. I think that's a terrible thing to have done, but I don't see that my family would be much different.

Mick now lives with another gay, who is a bit older than he is. He's a nice enough bloke. I go around there quite a bit, usually just to get out of the house, and maybe watch a video and have a few cans of beer.

I never noticed anything about Mick when we were younger. He was always a bit quiet, but he's a good friend. He never has a bad word to say about anybody.

I don't quite know how he became involved in the gay scene. He goes into town on a Saturday night to a gay bar, but I don't know how long he's been going there. I never ask him about that, because I don't really want to hear about it. I could never go to a gay bar – it would turn my stomach. I don't think it's natural. I wouldn't want to even think about having sex with another man.

Mick is about the only gay person I know, although there's probably other people on the estate who are gay too. I don't know about women much. I suppose it's easier for them because women are closer anyway. They can spend a lot of time together, and nobody would pass any comment.

I know that Mick is afraid of getting AIDS. He says that he'd hate to bring shame upon his family by dying from AIDS. He told me that he's been for a few tests, and that he was given the all-clear, but I know he worries. It only takes the once to get it. Everybody has to be careful about AIDS these days though, don't they? I don't sleep around now the way I used to when I was younger. I always use a condom now as well. I'm not afraid of AIDS, but I am more careful.

I heard that the law was changed about gay people last year. I never knew it was a crime. I think that if two people are equally consenting to sex, then it's their own private business.

Mick says that a gay person is just the same as any other person, except for who they are sexually attracted to – I am still thinking about that. I'd like to find out more about Mick's life – only so that I won't be ignorant.

As far as I'm concerned he's not harming anybody, so he's perfectly entitled to live his own life. I fee sorry for him because his family have turned their backs on him. He never mentions them, but it must really hurt him. He works in the civil service, so he's got a good enough job, and he doesn't do drugs or anything like that.

I hope that if I ever have kids that I wouldn't turn my back on one of them if they told me they were gay. I'd try to accept it, and I wouldn't let anyone put them down for it. There's much worse things that a child could tell its parents. I wouldn't care if gay people wanted to marry, or bring up kids. They couldn't do any better or worse than anybody else. Around my area, there are loads of single mothers. There's nothing but pushchairs on the streets. If a gay couple wanted to bring up kids, then why not?

LINDA CULLEN

My name is Linda Cullen. I am thirty years old and come from a middle-class family in south Co. Dublin.

I was twenty-three when I had my first relationship with a woman. It came as a huge surprise to me. I had been living as a fairly happy – probably very happy – very regular heterosexual up until then. I'd had boyfriends when I was in my teens and twenties; I'd had one happy long-term relationship for two years. Some of my relationships weren't good and some were good, and I didn't know any other way. Then at twenty-three my best friend and I fell in love with each other. It was like having lived all your life in one country, believing that this was all you could ask for, and then going to visit another country and discovering that there are other ways of living. As far as I am aware, my lesbianism wasn't something that was hidden inside me, waiting to burst out – it was something that just happened, and which I have never, ever regretted, even though that relationship turned out very badly.

When the relationship was failing, I told my mother, because I was so upset. I told her I was in love with a woman. Her only concerns were first, whether I was okay, and second, was I a lesbian? At the time I didn't have a clue what I was. All I knew was that this person was leaving me and I was devastated. I said to my mother, 'What does it matter what I am?' She just said, 'Well, Linda, it's a more difficult life than the other way.' She told me her only concern was for me and I believe that, because she has never been less than 100 per cent supportive of me always, to the extent that my partner and I lived with her for a period of time.

I think that the support of family and close friends is one of the most important things for someone coming out. It's desperately hard for those people who don't have it, and those who have come out despite that are braver than the rest of us put together. I also have full support from my brothers and the rest of my family, who have made me guardian or godmother, and in some cases both, to all their children, and who have done this since they've known I'm a lesbian. It doesn't bother them in the least. They regard myself and my partner as a stable happy couple they would be happy to have rear their children. They know who I am, and they love who I am.

The coming-out process was a bit arse about face for me. I had told a few friends about my relationship with this other woman before I told my mother, but I had never used the word 'lesbian'. I didn't know if I was lesbian or bisexual – I didn't know what I was at all. All I knew was that I loved this person. As a result of that relationship I wrote a novel called *The Kiss*. Although I had never said publicly I was a lesbian, in the papers or on the radio, or said what I was or wasn't, I more or less felt that it shouldn't be anyone else's concern. However, I feel differently now; I feel it's important to say you're a lesbian if you are a lesbian. But at the time it felt peculiar to be labelled a lesbian before I was aware that I was one, or before I had decided that this was the route my life was going to take. I think it's important to know that you can go all the way to twenty-three, thirty three, fifty-three – and then discover something else to change your mind. I'm not saying it's a choice; once you've been there I don't feel that you can go back. It would have been foolish for me to go back, and I didn't, and don't, want to.

A couple of things made me realise I was a lesbian. Firstly, four years ago I fell in love with another woman, whom I'd known for some time already, and we've lived together for most of the time since. We're very happy and very much part of my family. Our relationship is not shunned or ignored, and that's very important to me. I expect that she be invited to all family events in the way that my brothers' wives or girlfriends are, and she always has been; if not I would have been very, very upset, and rightly so.

The second thing that convinced me happened when I was in New York, making a documentary about Irish gays and lesbians who had been banned from marching in the St Patrick's Day parade with all the other Irish and quasi-Irish groups. Seeing how brave they were made me feel that it was time to say to myself, 'Look, you're a lesbian, you're pretty happy about it, so tell it like it is.' That's why I'm putting my name to this. I'm telling it like it is.

JAMES

I come from a fairly large family down the country. I was abused a lot at school. I knew I was gay from a young age, and I always felt okay about it. However, when I was bullied at school, I tried to reject my sexuality. I went out with girls, and tried to live a 'straight' life. I went to college when I left school, where I met a girl called Davina. We were going out together for a year, when I decided I should come out to her and tell her I was gay. She accepted my homosexuality, and when we left college, we went to London to live and work. We decided to have a non-monogamous relationship.

At this stage I considered myself bisexual. Davina and I had a very good sexual relationship, though I found it extremely difficult when she started going out with other men. At one point she moved back to Ireland for a few months, and it was during this time that I had my first gay relationship, and started to come out to my friends. Not one of them rejected me. Davina returned to London, and we rekindled our relationship. As a result of this, she became pregnant. This was a devastating blow to us both, but we were able to talk things over, and we decided to keep the baby.

Davina said that she would marry me – but only on condition that I would settle into a completely monogamous, heterosexual marriage, and that we would return to Ireland. I'm afraid that I couldn't agree to this, but I did want the best for both of us. So we went to counselling – but unfortunately it didn't help much.

This was a very isolating time for us. Her family didn't want to know us – they were a very rural family, with very traditional values. Davina and I became very close at this time, and our son was born in 1990. We were a family. We moved into a new flat. I found a very good job, and we were happy. The only downfall is that every weekend I went into London to have one-night stands with other gay men. I discussed these events very openly with Davina.

When our son was a year old, Davina started to go out socially again, and she met and became involved with a guy. She asked me to move out of the flat, which I did. I myself became involved with another man, but I really wasn't able to handle any relationship. I just needed very badly for someone to love me.

Davina's partner turned out to be violent, and indeed things became so bad that she fled to Ireland with our son. In 1992 I followed her. It was a difficult move, because I had no job and no friends, and I had to find somewhere to live. The one positive note was that I had access to my son again.

Now Davina is with another man, and they are very happy. Our son is now four years old. I usually have him with me for one week each month. We go to my parents' house. My mother is very supportive and very helpful. The rest of the family is accepting, apart from my father. I am in a relationship now myself with a man. My family have met him, and he has been integrated very well. I am involved in the gay community in Dublin. I feel very proud and very happy to be gay now. This is who I am, and I couldn't be anything else. I have grown in confidence over the past few years. I feel that I can hold my head as high as the next person.

I am glad that I have a son. I love him very much, and I am very proud of him. I love children. They bring so much pleasure into your life. They are a responsibility as well, but I wouldn't change my circumstances. I'm glad that I'm a father, and I think that any gay person who wishes to have children should be allowed to do so.

KAREN

A few years ago now a friend of mine came to visit me, and she was very upset. She could hardly speak to me because she was crying so hard. Eventually I managed to calm her down enough, and she began to tell me that she had discovered that her husband was gay, and had been gay all their married life. My friend was completely devastated. She had been married for a few years, and they have children. They had always had a good marriage. Her husband had a good job, a very good job, and they were a very nice family.

My friend had no idea that her husband was gay. He had never mentioned anything to her before. She simply couldn't take it in – it was too much for her. She said that she had been out one evening having a drink with a friend, and when she returned to the house she found her husband watching a gay film, and he was in a very excited state. She reckoned that he had been masturbating, and had obviously been very aroused by what he was watching. She immediately questioned her husband, and demanded to know what was going on. He didn't even attempt to conceal anything. He told her there and then that he was gay, and that he had always been gay. He told her that sometimes when he would go to Dublin to watch a football match, he would go to gay bars, and he would have a one-night stand with a man. He had been doing this before they were even married.

My friend couldn't believe she had been deceived in this way. She was angry at what he had been doing, and especially that they had children together. What if he had caught AIDS? What did he intend doing now? They had a very good home, and she certainly didn't want to leave it. They sat up all night, and at the end of all their discussion, they decided that what would do to suit everybody would be to continue to live under the same roof. He had a very high-profile job, and he needed to have the marriage in order to present a good family front. My friend feels that perhaps this was the only reason he did get married.

The children are still too young to know or understand what is going on. But it makes her feel cheap and used. She feels like she is only a possession – a necessary thing in his life. She has put so much into the marriage and into bringing up the children. She keeps everything looking very well, and she herself always looks immaculate. But there is so much hidden behind all the apparent glamour of her life.

I know my friend's husband very well too. We used to go out for meals with them quite regularly, and we'd sometimes go out for a few drinks. Since I discovered that he is gay, I can't say that I feel any differently towards him, but then I'm not married to him. I feel sorry for my friend. I don't know how she will fare trying to keep up appearances. A person can only do that for so long.

I have children myself, and if one of them were gay, I'd like to support them as much as possible. I think that a family should always see each other through all the bad times, because we all need support at one time or another. However, I would find it difficult if my child was gay, and they brought home another gay friend, or a partner, for us to meet. I'm not so sure that I could handle that situation. I'd imagine that would be a difficult experience for any parent.

MICHELLE

My brother is gay. He is twenty-three, and he still lives at home with us.

He hasn't actually told me that he is gay, but he told my mother about a year ago, and my mother was so shocked that she told me.

One day my brother sat down to have a cup of coffee with my mother, and he said that he had something to tell her. He told her that he had always known that he was gay, but that it had taken him ages to get the courage to tell my parents. He said that he wanted to get used to the gay lifestyle himself first, before he said anything to anybody else.

My brother is two years older than I am, and we've always got on very well. He was always a bit quiet at home, and he was never interested in football much. He never went out with girls either, but we always just put that down to his quiet nature. He had friends, though. They used to sit around the home listening to music, and eating whatever they could find. He was never that good at school, and he left when he was sixteen. He was lucky enough to be taken on by a local company as an apprentice electrician.

He is a real easygoing kind of person. He never gets angry about anything. He just lives his life quietly. At the weekend he usually goes off into town to have a few drinks. We never knew though until recently that he goes to gay bars. He doesn't go out at all during the week. He just sits at home and watches TV.

My parents are over the initial shock now. They don't say much about my brother. They hardly mention him much at all in conversation. But it was like living in a war zone when he first told them. My mum and dad both blamed each other for what had happened. They tried to understand where they had gone wrong, but they knew really that nothing had gone wrong, and it was nobody's fault.

After a few months, they calmed down, and they talked to my brother. During this time myself and the rest of my brothers and sisters were told nothing. We didn't know what was going on. We thought that maybe he'd been caught taking drugs or something. When mum told me that he was gay, I was really shocked. It was the last thing I expected to hear. I have no objections to gay people, but it was still a shock to me, because this was my own brother.

I think it's because you have lived with someone all your life, and then suddenly they turn out to be somebody different, it takes time to start to relate to the person in a new way. I still like my brother as a person, but I wish that he would tell me himself that he is gay. He still doesn't know that I know about him.

My only fear is that he will get AIDS. I wish that I could talk to him about the risks involved with unprotected sex, but then I suppose that's really his own business.

I would hate to see anything happening to him, because he's a really nice person. I don't know if he's in a relationship or not. He doesn't bring his friends back to the house any more. I think that my parents asked him not to. He never really talks about where he goes, or who he's with.

Recently, he's been talking about leaving home.

Maybe he finds it too confining, and that he can't be himself. I hope that he always keeps in touch with me, and that one day we can share this side of his life. He is my brother and I hope that I'll always be a good friend to him.

PAULINE

I am the mother of a gay woman. My daughter is now nineteen. She only told me within the last year that she is gay. I still haven't come to terms with it. I think that maybe it's just a phase that she is going through, and I hope that she'll grow out of it.

I don't want my daughter to live her life as a gay woman. She's a very attractive girl, and I'm sure she'd have no problem finding a boyfriend. She's at college now, so she must be mixing with lots of boys who would be suitable for her. I can't understand why she has chosen to be gay. She has always had everything she has ever wanted from her father and myself. I don't understand why she would want to throw it all back in our face. We have always tried to give her the best, and we have been good parents to her.

We couldn't have our own children, and when we had been married for seven years we decided to adopt. We went through all the procedures, and eventually we received word about Bernie. It was the happiest day of our lives. We brought her home when she was only four weeks old. She was everything to us. We invited our families over to the house to celebrate with us, and everybody thought that she was really something special. We told Bernie from an early stage that she was adopted because we thought it would be better that way. She grew up accepting it, and she was always a delight to us. She was an only child, so she was always quite spoiled. She was a very outgoing girl, and always out and about with friends. I was happy to see her enjoying herself. She grew up the same as any other child. She went to school, she had a few accidents over the years, falling off a horse, and breaking her arm ... the usual ups and downs of any childhood.

When she was thirteen, my husband started sexually abusing her – which I only found out about two years ago. My husband apparently started to talk to her about sexual activities, asking her had she ever done any of these things with a boy. After a while he started to demonstrate to her, which started from touching her, all the way through to full sexual intercourse. I had no idea that anything like this was going on. I was usually working when all these horrible things were taking place. I still can't take it in. I can't believe what he did to his own daughter.

This behaviour went on for about four years. I never even noticed any difference in my daughter's behaviour. She was as outgoing as ever. She didn't suddenly start drinking or anything. I don't know how she survived so well. My husband used to be away from home sometimes on business, and he would always bring Bernie back very expensive toys and presents. She never seemed to like them, and now I can understand why. She felt that she was being bought, and that she felt dirty. I find it very upsetting to talk about this. I blame myself for not seeing what was happening.

My husband died two years ago. He had a massive heart attack. It was only then that Bernie told me about him. We have come through it all now. Bernie and I are very close. She lives at home with me, and really we have become best friends.

Bernie went for counselling after my husband died. She still goes once a month, but she has talked through a lot of things now. Apparently she discussed her sexuality with her counsellor. I have talked to the counsellor myself a few times. She has helped us both very much. Bernie has said that she has always been attracted to other women, and she has never found men attractive. She says that she has not been put off men by what has happened to her with her father. Today she seems to be a much happier girl. She has started to go to a gay bar at weekends, but she has never mentioned that she has become involved with anybody. I'm sure she would tell me if she did, because she always tells me who she meets, and how her night was.

I still feel shocked that Bernie is gay. I wanted to give her so much in her life, and I was looking forward to her wedding day. I can't pretend that this is what I want for her, because it's not. However, I do love her, and I don't want this to come between us. We have been through so much over the last few years, and I'm sure that we'll get through this as well.

MARK

One of my earliest and most vivid memories is one of watching naked men showering. I was intensely fascinated but at the age of about four I didn't know why.

I was the eldest of two sons. My proud dad was the captain of a rugby team (hence the access to the men's shower area) and my mum, like all mothers, had a very clear view as to how she expected us to turn out, from marriage to careers and Catholicism.

I felt different from my friends as I grew up and I feared the future. Everyone else seemed to have built-in automatic motivation for the things their life ahead held for them and I just didn't feel a part of it. Throughout my time in secondary school, harsh criticism from my parents for me to be more motivated and grown-up made me become insular and alienated. My only real interest was in watching or adoring the guy I was in love with at the time.

My grandmother lived with us and I became very close to her. Her wit, wisdom and acceptance of me for who I was made me feel secure. By the time I was sixteen I was very unhappy. I felt trapped inside a shy person full of nervous energy which I rarely managed to express. Whenever I was asked any personal questions, my muddled perception of homosexuality and the hatred of it filled my mind. At seventeen I went to college and my parents were concerned that I was still so moody and such a loner. My brother (a year younger than me) had long since passed me out regarding going out at night, girls, drinking et cetera.

One Friday night my parents and brother had gone out and I watched *The Late Late Show*. It was about homosexuality and it had real gay men in the audience. Some were gorgeous, some spoke out really well, but most of all they were normal people demanding equal rights.

After a long silence my grandmother said that they were different from us but difference should be accepted. I found myself saying that I was different too. Someone finally really knew me. I had always thought that someone knowing would be enough to

make me happy, but suddenly being gay was
something real that I had to find a way to express and
explore. When my grandmother died a couple of
months later I knew I couldn't let myself be isolated
once more. She had lived her life completely and it
was time for me to live mine.

I went to the next meeting of the Lesbian and Gay
Youth Group. I loved it. For the first time I could see a
clear future with promise and challenge. I made some
great friends and soon found myself a boyfriend,
Chris. My parents were curious as to the change in my
character but I was afraid to tell as I knew that to have
a gay son would horrify them. I wanted to live and
enjoy my lifestyle before I had to defend it. My parents
were less than enamoured with Chris (his pierced nose
and pink mohican may have had something to do
with this). I felt I had some catching up to do in the
area of sex. The thought of it seemed natural but I
couldn't visualise two guys together sexually. I got a
loan of a gay porn video and hid it under the
floorboards of my bedroom. My brother found it and
left it in the video recorder! The next morning dad
played the tape. He went crazy and stormed up to my
room and threw the tape at me demanding to know
why I'd left a 'filthy queer video' for him to see, and
said, 'I want everything queer out of this house!' I said
that he would have to throw me out too. I left the
house and went to the youth group. A special meeting
for parents who had accepted their child's homosexuality was being held. I sat there feeling immense guilt,
confusion and anger, convinced that my family would
never accept me – the happy families there seemed a
million miles away from mine.

The next few months were absolute hell, a

whirlpool of rancour and recrimination. I couldn't see any light at the end of the tunnel. It's scary trying to defend a lifestyle that you've barely experienced. I felt permanently on trial with the most private areas of my life exposed, and I felt guilty for putting the people I loved through so much pain.

After a summer abroad I returned home and things were a lot calmer, so I made sure that they didn't get any more shocks. I didn't bring any more punks home and wasn't questioned about my activities.

For the next year my parents were distant and tense, with mealtime gatherings resembling something from a David Lynch film. Gradually the situation improved until this Christmas Day, when my parents returned home early and were very friendly to my friend Gene. Then my mum gave me a wink and asked Gene to stay for Christmas dinner. I collapsed back into my chair. My mum still doesn't really believe that I'm not going out with Gene, but I'm not complaining. They're trying to show acceptance, which is as brilliant as it was unanticipated.

Being out as gay is one part of my identity, a part I am proud of. Coming out is something you hope to get through with some of your mental health intact, but you end up with a whole lot less emotional energy to put into other things in your life.

Suzy

To refer to my childhood as a sheltered is probably an understatement. While my upbringing wasn't quite the Opus Dei, staunchly Catholic type, it wasn't far from it. I was totally unaware of the reasons for my alienation from other young people, both male and female. I was sheltered from the real world, although intelligent, willing to learn and aware of the world and issues in it. I knew I was different from the heterosexual 'normality' expected from both myself and all those around me. When I was fourteen I was yearning for knowledge about my body and those other 'forbidden facts of life'. I told my father that I was not going to be the same as other young women. I wasn't going to get married, have 2.4 children and be an adoring and submissive wife. Dad, in his fatherly wisdom, said that I didn't know what I was talking about and that I was too young to know otherwise.

I was a Catholic, though, and loved religion, the ceremony and my participation within it. I read at Mass, and later went on to be the youngest Minister of the Eucharist in my parish, and probably the most pious young person in my year at school. I had great problems at school though; I was different, too grown up for my age and still none the wiser about sex and sexuality. I wanted to be closer to my female classmates. I had massive crushes on my teachers, part-icularly my English teacher who was a butch hockey-playing goddess I would have done anything for. I didn't know that lesbians existed then. Being gay was a male disease to me. I was instructed and believed that gay men were dirty and demented, and that AIDS was the wrath of God. I did not question but, during my Leaving Cert., I fought with my parents about divorce, abortion and contraception and the problems I had with the Catholic Church's teaching on these issues. This began a change in my thinking.

I finished school at sixteen and begged a male acquaintance to come to my debs – all to keep up the show of normality. I still didn't realise that I was a lesbian. After a year of torment with my lack of success in the dating game I left for England. Still a young virginal Irish Catholic girl, I was shocked at the new culture. I was homesick, lonely and angry at my thoughts about being with other women. I began to read all around me while studying books about assertiveness, the female orgasm, relationships and psychology. The newfound knowledge in what my mother called a pagan country began to take effect. I came across a book on teenage sexual experiences. These weren't ordinary teenagers – they were young lesbians and gay men. After a rapid self-diagnosis, I rang the London Lesbian and Gay Switchboard and found out about a local lesbian and gay youth group. It was run by a youth worker and I arranged to see her before I went to the group. It was a great release: two and half hours of tears and laughter and, above all, a great feeling of not being 'strange' any more.

I told no one at work about my newfound happiness. I went to youth group meetings and continued going to counselling. I ventured out on to the scene and loved and hated it. I fell in love – well, it was really lust. Then I met Fran, another Irish girl. We met in the launderette. She wasn't anything special to look at, but then neither was I. We were both at the same college but doing different things. At first, we became great friends. We were both loners and, although on different courses, found that we had a lot in common. It was weeks before we both realised that we were more alike than we first thought. Our love deepened and we accepted each other for what we were. Bliss wasn't the word. Our relationship lasted three years and was strung over hundreds of miles and many visits and extravagant phone calls after I came home. Dad wasn't so happy about my new friend and my love of life and all things female. He rejected me for many months, tried to get me to change and refused to understand that my relationship was not just a phase.

My secret life continued. I began working with young people. I still loved Fran dearly but the distance between us grew too much. I told very few of my friends about my love. The Church still mattered to me but I knew that they would not accept me for who I really was. I argued with members of the clergy about the Church's attitude to lesbians and gays. I had no contact with other lesbians and gays while I was in Dublin. I stayed in the closet for fear of persecution because of my work with young people. I wanted to rebel, to speak out and change people's attitudes to lesbians and gays. I wanted to add my voice to the growing call for changes in the law, but the attitudes of the Church and its people stopped me. A job interview and a vicious Vatican statement (Ratzinger et al.) changed all that.

My work with young people continues although the Church chucked me out and I duly snubbed them. Now I am busy being gay and making up for the years of silence and the torment of my youth when I didn't know what being a lesbian was and just knew I was different.

MARK

My sister is gay. She is twenty-three years old. We are very close, and I think that she's great to have the courage to live as a gay person. There are only the two of us in the family. She is two years younger than I am and we have always got on well together. Susan is more outgoing than I am; she is the kind of person who can talk to anybody about anything. I'm not like that. I get tongue-tied, and can barely put a few words together. Neither of us live at home any more. I am married now, with two kids of my own, and Susan has her own house. We are both close to our parents, though. We usually come together on a Sunday for dinner. It's always good to be with the family once a week, and to have a chat. We are all trying to create nice gardens at the moment, so that is this month's topic of conversation. Mum and Dad are great at giving a hand, and passing on all sorts of useful tips to us. They are a very gentle, caring couple, although they can both have a fierce temper at times too – usually when somebody has let them down in some way. Susan has told all of us that she is gay. She told us after dinner one Sunday, because she said that she wanted us all to be together. I think that it was a very brave thing to do. I didn't feel shocked or anything; I just thought that this is who she is, and if she's happy about it, then that's okay. Mum and Dad took it very well too. They asked her a few questions, and they said that if she was happy, then that's all that mattered. They are very easygoing people, and they are not prejudiced against anybody. They say that life is too short for all that kind of thing, and I think that it's a very sensible view.

Our extended family knows about Susan as well. One of my uncles isn't too happy about it but everybody else is fine. However, my uncle has never said anything personally to Susan. Susan tried to explain the situation to our granny, and she said that the main things in life are health and happiness, but I'm still not sure that she knows what being gay is all about. But then she is more than seventy-four years old, and things like homosexuality would never have been spoken about when she was younger.

Susan doesn't really go to gay bars or anything like that. She says that they only help to create a ghetto mentality. She says that if she wants to have a drink somewhere, than she will go to any pub. She has met someone, though. I think that they met at college. They have been seeing each other for just over a year now. I don't know how serious things are. They only see each other at weekends. I don't feel that I have a problem with Susan having a girlfriend. I don't want to know what she does with her sex life, and I'm sure she doesn't want to know about mine either. My wife, Liz, gets on well with Susan. They sometimes go out for a drink together. Liz doesn't have a problem with Susan being gay. She doesn't have a problem with Susan baby-sitting for the kids either. I've read in magazines that gay people are often kept away from children, because they're seen as perverts. I think that is a ridiculous thing to say. My sister is not perverted. She is gay. She is attracted to other women and not just any women, but other gay women. Susan is studying to be a teacher at the moment. She has always wanted to be a teacher. She loves children, and should be a very good teacher.

As far as I'm concerned, Susan is a very important part of my life, and I wouldn't want her to change anything about her life. She is happy being who she is, so surely that can't be wrong.

JOSEPHINE

I am seventy-three years of age, and I'd like to tell you about my nephew, Dermot, who is gay. He is my brother's son, and lives in England. My brother died earlier this year. He and his wife had two children, Dermot and Sandra. They used to come over to visit us from England very regularly. We were never a really close family, but we did get on really well when we were together.

When Dermot was younger, he was a great swimmer. He was really exceptionally good, but apart from that he was the same as any other young person of his age. Anyhow, when Dermot was around fourteen years of age, suddenly they stopped coming to visit us. There was no explanation or correspondence or any such thing. We didn't know at that time that Dermot was gay, though funnily enough my husband had commented to me on how feminine he was.

When Dermot was in his mid-twenties, he started to drink very heavily. He actually became a chronic alcoholic, and he put his parents through a very bad time. He completely disrupted the household, he stole money to buy drink, and he was always being brought home by the police when they would find him in a drunken state in the street.

I think now that my brother and his wife were ashamed of this happening in the family, and so they decided to cope with it by cutting themselves off from the rest of us.

My brother had a friend who had connections with a private clinic for rehabilitating alcoholics, and they were fortunate enough to find a place for Dermot there. At that time Dermot had some very good jobs, and he moved in very upmarket circles. He had a friend who was a dentist, and he had also been supplying Dermot with drugs, so when Dermot went into the clinic he was in need of some very serious help. He had to stay there for quite a long time, and during this time he was not allowed any visitors. It was while he was in the clinic that it came out that he was gay. This was a big factor in his drinking. He had been trying to conceal his gayness, and had ended up with a serious drinking problem. His parents found this news very hard to take. They had already been put through so much by their son, and this was only something else for them to feel ashamed about.

While all of this was going on with Dermot, my brother and his wife also had problems with their daughter. She had dropped out of college, and had moved in with an Indian guy. She lived with this guy for thirteen years, and they had two children. This too was a major disappointment to my brother and his wife. They felt that they had put everything into their children, and the children had let them down by not living up to their expectations.

A few years later my brother was very ill in hospital with cancer. Dermot started to visit his father in the hospital, and he was very caring indeed towards him. By this time, Dermot had managed to stay off the drink, and he now had a little business for himself, and lived in a nice apartment. He also had a partner, although none of us knew this until the day of his father's funeral.

Sadly, to this day Dermot's mother no longer keeps in touch with us. She seems to have gone into herself, and cannot face the truth about her children.

For myself, I believe that people are born gay. I think that we have to accept that. In my younger days we had never even heard of sex, never mind gay people! I have always had a broad outlook on life. I think that I learned much of that from my own mother. Also, most of my working life was spent working in the unions, and doing that kind of work you gain much experience in learning about people. I came across harassment in the workplace, for example, but we didn't call it that then. I think that life teaches us to be broad-minded as we live more.

MARY CARTHY

My son died of AIDS four years ago. He was only twenty-nine years of age. He had been sick for a long time, but he didn't tell us. He didn't want to worry the family. However, as time went on, he became very sick, and had to be taken into hospital. He was very stressed out, because he was worrying about hurting and shaming the family. He knew that there was a huge stigma attached to any person who had AIDS, and he wanted to protect us from that.

After a while, we took Joe home with us. They had been trying to give him different medications at the hospital, but nothing was working, so we all decided that it would be better if Joe could live out the final weeks of his life surrounded by his own friends and family. Joe was very nervous about coming home, but I told him that we all knew that he was gay, and that he had AIDS, and I reassured him that everything was okay.

The house was always full of visitors – everyone came to see Joe. Many nights I would sleep beside Joe, and we would talk for hours. We talked so freely about everything. It was a very special time for both of us. One night I was talking to him, and he told me that he was very sorry for bringing this on me. He told me that he loved us very much. These are words any mother is delighted to hear.

When Joe died, we were there around his bed. He mouthed to us that he loved us, and he closed his eyes. It was a very beautiful and peaceful moment.

Joe told his brother that he had made his own funeral arrangements. He had asked us would we mind if his gay friends attended his funeral, and actually I don't know how I would have coped without their support. They were the most caring group of people you could ever meet.

Joe always lived his life to the full. He loved clothes and holidays. Even when he was away on holidays, he would always call home to ask us how we were. He was so considerate and caring.

I always knew that he was gay – a mother always knows these things about her children. Nothing was ever said between us, but I knew. It wasn't a disappointment to me. I had brought him into the world, and I loved him, because he was my son. I know that some gay people are let down by their families, because they cannot accept that their child is gay, but I think that's a very sad situation.

My son was always respectful in his behaviour in our company. I never once felt ashamed of him.

I would say to any parent that having a gay child is no problem. I know that parents would wish that their child was heterosexual, but there is no reason why they cannot be loved for who they are.

AIDS was still a stigma when Joe died. But we were never afraid of getting AIDS. We washed our son and took care of him. You can't catch AIDS from these things.

Today, I put my belief in God. My consolation is that I believe that my son is in Heaven. I used to worry that my son would be alone in the world if anything happened to either of us. I never thought that Joe would die first. The pain at the loss of my son never goes away, but as time goes on, I'm learning to cope. I'd love to put my arms around Joe one more time.

When I talk on the radio or to the press now about AIDS, I do it for my son. This is what Joe would have wanted.

MAUREEN

My name is Maureen, and I am seventeen years old. I come from an ordinary housing estate on the north-side of Dublin. I live with my mother, who is a lesbian.

I've never really talked about my mother before, but it's mainly because I feel that it's nobody's business. I'm not ashamed of my mother, nor do I feel embarrassed about her. I love her very much. She's a good and caring person – although it's only quite recently that I've come to see this.

My father lived with us until nearly four years ago. He is a really good person, and I live with him at weekends. He is an electrician and loves his work, although he doesn't earn very much, compared to some people. But he has always given me everything I've needed, and every year, he brings us on a great holiday, usually to Spain. My mum never worked, except at home. She is very houseproud, and is always cleaning the house from top to bottom.

I always thought that we had a happy family life, although when I was younger, I often wished that I had a brother or sister for company. My mother has always had lots of friends, and the house was always full of neighbours, chatting and drinking tea. People don't have much where we live, so the neighbours are always borrowing a few bob from each other, and sharing around whatever few cigarettes they had, and even potatoes, bread and milk. So there was always someone in the house handing in something or borrowing something or just calling round for a chat.

I only discovered that my mother is a lesbian three years ago, when I was fourteen. She sat down with me one night after dinner, and told me all about it. Apparently, my mother became sexually involved with one of her friends. They have been friends for ages, and she lives on the next road from us. She is married too, but her husband drinks a lot, so she always spent loads of time in our house. I don't really know all the details about how things started, but I know they have been having a relationship for a few years now. My mother told me that's why she split up with my dad, although my dad doesn't talk to me about it. She told me that she has always been attracted to women, but she was always too shy to do anything about it. She got married because that's what all her friends were doing, and she had known my dad since they were children.

I don't really want to go into my mother's private life too much, but I think that she is happy with her lesbian relationship. She keeps it fairly quiet because people in our area might become very bitchy towards her if they knew she was gay.

I love my mother and my father very much. I'm sorry that they've had to split up, but I understand why they did. I live with my mother and I wouldn't leave her. I know that she would never hurt me or my father for the world.

I've read bits in the newspapers recently about lesbian mothers, and many people seem to think they shouldn't be allowed to have children. My mother is a good parent. She is honest, loving and she always makes sure I'm well dressed and have money to go out with my friends. Having a lesbian for a mother isn't going to make me a lesbian too. I have a boyfriend, and I'm definitely heterosexual. I talk to my mother about my boyfriend, and how we are getting on. She's a good friend to me, as well as a mother.

I like my mother's girlfriend. I've known her for years. She has always been nice to me, and she has always taken an interest in what I'm doing – at school, or with my friends, and so on. Apart from my mother and her girlfriend, I don't really know many gay people ... or I probably do, it's not the kind of thing you talk about where I live, because you wouldn't want to go out of your way to make yourself a scapegoat.

NOELLE

I am in my mid-forties and live in Dublin. I come from a strict, Roman Catholic, upper-middle-class background. My father was a medical doctor who later became actively involved in the pro-life movement. I grew up in a house of brothers, and my memories are of a happy childhood full of laughter and fun, spent playing with my brothers and their friends. My father used to bring me with him on his rounds – to homes, hospitals, clinics and even an army barracks. However, when I was ten, my father told me that because I was a girl I could no longer go with him on his army visits. I was extremely upset and did not understand the reason for this sudden change.

At about the same time my mother tried to select my friends for me as she did not approve of me playing with the boys, nor with certain girls. The girls she chose for me to play with were definitely not the tomboy type, so I quickly understood that being a tomboy was not acceptable. I think it is ironic that all of these 'tomboys' are living very straight lives – many of them are TV and radio presenters, and successful women in the media and other public areas.

At thirteen I was packed off to boarding school. I felt very confused by this and could not understand why I had to be sent away 'to be a lady'. It was probably to teach me discipline and manners. However, for me boarding school was a good experience. The nuns were strict but kind and instilled in me a strong sense of social justice and equality, and a good grounding in world affairs. I developed a questioning and inquiring mind which has stayed with me since.

After leaving school I continued to have a great social life, with lots of boyfriends; within four years I received three marriage proposals. But I was not interested in settling down to marriage in my early twenties, though back then, in the late sixties, marriage was expected to come after school for a woman.

When I was twenty-two I was told that I had to have a major and urgent operation for cancer of the throat area and I was sent off to a specialist clinic in London. I where to go for expert medical help. My treatment was successful but the experience of looking death in the face changed me dramatically. From then on I lived life fast and to the full and never looked back.

I remember one evening in my parents' house watching *The Late Late Show* on TV and a group of very articulate, strident women were talking about women's lot in life and how we were being unfairly and unequally treated. It brought feminism into our sitting-rooms for the first time in Ireland. I tried to listen but my father and brothers were roaring ridicule at these women, whilst my mother laughed. The programme had a profound effect on my thoughts and I felt that I should have the guts to support these women – but how?

By now I had a job which I loved and was embarking on a successful career. I married a man I had known, cared about and respected for many years. Our families knew each other and were very pleased. With hindsight I think we were nervous about marriage but we both wanted a child.

However, I had to leave my job because of a marriage bar. Shortly afterward my employers wanted me back, so I became the first married woman to work for this trade union. But then I had to leave again because there was a pregnancy bar – by now I was beginning to understand a lot about discrimination.

Once again the union called me back to work when my baby was a couple of months old, and sent me to college for further training. I was now working, studying and feeding the baby as well as cooking the meals at home. Although my husband was fantastic with the baby and was, and is, a very good and gentle man, in those days men had no part nor hand in housework and I was left to do it all and consequently collapsed on my feet with sheer exhaustion.

At this time student sit-ins and uprisings were taking place all over the world, and civil rights and black-power movements were emerging. In Ireland the first report of the Commission on the Status of Women had been published. I encountered daily this new wave of feminism in my work. The family, welfare, education and health systems were being analysed and criticised by women who felt strongly enough about such issues to demand change. During all this time my husband was not working, so it made sense to me that he should take care of our baby son while I worked. I began to feel trapped and unhappy with my lot. I was not prepared to give up my job and career but at the same time I just could not work inside and outside the home.

As I was deeply unhappy and the marriage was simply not working, I left our comfortable lifestyle and moved into a bare flat on my own, leaving my son with his father as I felt he could and would do a much better job of minding our child.

Later one evening I went to a party and met a woman to whom I immediately felt attracted. I was told she was a lesbian. It was not a shocking experience for me – I was a little nervous at first, of course, but it was a very natural encounter which evolved into a relationship. However, the implications were to be terrifying. I had never experienced this attraction. In all my life, except for maybe one experimental advance made to me on holidays by a 'straight' woman, I had never come across any form of lesbianism, nor did I recognise it as such at the time.

Once my husband realised the marriage was over

we talked about a separation. I suggested we go for joint custody of our child and he seemed agreeable.

The next piece is difficult and very painful for me to recount.

I had been made redundant and was now living on the dole, I was put in touch with the Free Legal Aid people and a solicitor was arranged for me through them. I learnt that my case was going to the High Court as my husband wanted a Divorce a Mensa et Thoro.

Both parties met in a large solicitors' office in the centre of Dublin. After a brief discussion, I said I wanted only joint custody – no money, no part of the family home. I wanted it settled fairly and without any animosity, and this I thought was what my husband wanted and had agreed to.

I was left in a room on my own while my appointed solicitor and senior counsel discussed my case with my husband's legal team. What felt like hours passed. I had run out of cigarettes. A cleaning woman came into the room and said, 'Love, you are in deep trouble. They are all talking about you over there, and it does not look good for you. They have a lot of personal information about you and you should be very careful about what you say.' She then ran over the road to a hotel to get me cigarettes.

A few hours later, my legal team came bustling into the room. My barrister stood and, staring at the wall, said in a loud lecturing voice that I was being accused of having affairs and that my husband was going for sole custody of our child as I was not a fit mother. On the advice of his legal team and family he would fight for sole custody. I might even lose access to my child. My barrister threw my file on the solicitor's desk, said that he felt personally disgusted and wanted nothing more to do me, and walked out the door. My solicitor stared down at her desk as she suggested that I should rethink my position, and that she too wanted nothing to do with my case which, if I contested, would now end up publicly in the High Court, along with the Divorce a Mensa et Thoro. I had no idea what was happening to me, what was going on. I left their office feeling completely alone.

I walked over to a pub where I had arranged to meet some people, and sat in the snug in shock. A woman, a complete stranger, was looking at me and she said, 'You look as though you have just seen a ghost. Do you want to talk?' I said no, and told her she would not want to talk to me if she knew me. She said, 'Why, have you killed somebody?' I said, 'No, worse.' She laughed and said, 'Try me.' At her insistence and promise that she would never repeat what I told her or, if it was my wish, that she would never talk to me about it again, I did.

Marie was shocked, not at me but at the way I had been treated by my own legal advisers. She insisted that I hold my trust in her until the following Monday morning, as she wanted to get advice from some high-up legal contacts she had. She kept her word and made a call to a prominent senior counsel who advised caution in going to the High Court – the scandal, my career, my family, blackmail et cetera – but suggested that I get fresh legal advice, fast. The SC felt that I should get my legal team to apologise to me and stated that he was willing to personally make a complaint to the Bar against the team, thus forcing them to take my case. Marie guided me through the legal mire.

In the event I had no choice but to go to the High

Court and I was determined to fight for joint custody. I was told by another solicitor that I was being watched by a private investigator and that my phone was tapped. You see, I was up against the best legal team that money could buy. My own family had already turned their backs on me after the separation, and the only other support I had was the comradeship of the women's movement in which I was now involved. But none of these women knew of my personal plight.

When the case came to court my (free) legal team, made up of the same solicitor and a barrister, told me that they were saying nothing in my defence and that if I wanted to see my child again I was to say nothing even if asked by the judge. They convinced me that anything I said would weaken my position. At one point the judge looked in horror at me and called me forward (with one of my legal team in hot pursuit) to his desk. He leaned over and whispered, 'What is going on here? Do you know what is happening, are you aware of what is going to happen to you?' One solicitor (whom I had never seen before) pinched my arm in warning to say nothing. The judge noticed and told him to step back. I looked into the judge's eyes and did not know what to do or who to trust. He said, 'Do you want to come to my room alone where we can talk in private?' I was so scared, I said no. He said, 'Well, I don't know what they have threatened you with or what you have done, but it could not be worse than what you have been offered. I cannot help you if you won't talk.' My own legal team did not tell me that the 'deal' had already been done and that I was being offered access to my son for one hour a week under supervision. That is what I left the court with that day – all arranged for me by others.

I walked away. My legal team disappeared. I saw my husband and his lawyers in the distance. I walked a mile through that round room out on to the streets on my own.

Soon afterwards my car was stopped at traffic lights and I saw my son walking with his granny. He saw me and screamed, 'Mammy, mammy, mammy.' His granny looked around, saw me and dragged my child away by the hand. My son was hysterical and crying. It broke my heart. I pulled the car in and cried till I was sick.

The woman I was involved with at this time left because she was so scared of being tainted by my court appearance. I was completely alone.

The first year was awful. I would have preferred at times not to see my son at all than just to have that tense hour a week with him. But once the dust had settled and time passed my husband began to ignore the custody ruling and I got to see my child more and more. After a while he came to me after school every day and then we would go away on holidays each year together.

My son knows I am a lesbian. I have never hidden it from him. We talk about it naturally. When I lost him I made two promises: one, that I would never say anything against his dad or his family or force him to choose between us in any way; and two, that I would never lie to him no matter how painful it was for either of us. I know that coming to terms with me and my sexuality has been and will continue to be very difficult at times for him; he faces and feels the prejudice every day. I remember one awful time, in France, when he was being really bolshy and he said I did not care at all about him. We exploded at each other, but when we

115

talked I found out that he never knew that I had lost custody of him; he thought I had just walked away. He was very upset and angry and wanted to lash out. I convinced him that there was no point; the hurt had been done and the best he could do was try to understand the circumstances, the times and attitudes and learn from it. Our hearts were broken at the disclosure and he left for Belgium on a train. I remember his saying, 'Mum, I love you,' and my heart going out to him. The idea of him going away alone on a long train journey with this information was so painful.

Another time, some years later, I visited my brother in Australia. My brother is homophobic and very macho and from the moment we met he kept baiting me about homosexuality. It was clear he had either heard about me or presumed. It was awful: my brother tried to push my son and me apart. I ended up leaving the house and my son insisted on coming with me.

My son is an adult now, and we are good friends most of the time. He has turned out, by all accounts, to be a very balanced person. He is also very caring and gentle. He is very clear and comfortable about his own sexuality, which is heterosexual, and he has a long-term girlfriend. I am also very fond of his father, whom I would also consider a good friend now.

From my experiences I have learned a great deal about prejudice – not only other people's prejudice towards me, but also my own. I have also learned that there is power in money and information. I was saved when young because my father had the knowledge and connections to get me the medical treatment I needed; without the help of Marie and her legal contacts I would have lost even more in my court case.

Looking back on my life I can recall, with pain,

pleasure and passion, two very important and lasting lesbian relationships. One relationship ended because our work took us to different countries. When my second and last relationship split up it was a very difficult time for me. I was devastated when it ended. I still feel the pain, even now, at the loss of that relationship and friendship.

Essentially I felt betrayed. She was pursuing or having another relationship which she vehemently denied and said, and made me feel, that I was paranoid and mad – and I know I behaved that way as a result. Our relationship was going through a bad patch. I wanted and would have done anything to make it work, but when your partner's attention and emotions are elsewhere there is nothing you can do only make a bad situation worse. You are just not wanted, you are in the way and become an irritant. In my case most people who knew us in Ireland believed I was wrong and imagining things and I am sure they thought no wonder she wanted out of a relationship with this upset person which I became. Later when I was told, and she could no longer deny it, her defence was the relationship had ended and it was none of my business.

When a relationship ends for one person it has ended for the two unknown mostly to the other person (myself in this case). I often think that the end of such a relationship, for the one left behind, is worse than the bereavement experienced by death because you know this person still exists and are apprehensive of the pain caused by the constant possibility of running into them publicly with the new lover who once never existed. It can take a long time to understand why the person who leaves is so angry

117

because they feel the need to justify their actions and they have lost too.

But as time passes I can see her pain too and the impossible situation we both found ourselves in and the hurt that was caused. Now I wish her happiness and health. Maybe I am ready to forgive. We are both difficult women and won't change – but maybe someday we might be able to talk and laugh again but at a distance – hopefully before we are in our graves.

I think it's very hard to be in a gay relationship. They are very difficult relationships to cultivate and to maintain, particularly between lesbians – and particularly with other women whose stories are like mine. But then many people, and not just gay people, experience the pain of a separation, like a death, in their lives, except that we lesbians have to do it privately and alone.

I feel that Maureen Gaffney put it very well when she wrote in *The Irish Times* that, 'because they [lesbians] are women, strong attachments are important. Because they are lesbians, forging a non-traditional image of strength and independence is also vital to their identity. With both partners having the same needs, many lesbian couples find it difficult to keep a balance between attachments and autonomy...perhaps because of the very high expectations lesbian women bring to their intimate relationships.'

I made the choice not to come out to my parents, or publicly. They knew that I was into feminism, but they never knew that I was a lesbian. Why should I bring this on their lives? I also know that my life would have been made even more difficult by them: my father once publicly said that lesbians should be taken out of society and treated medically and that he, as a doctor, felt they were no better than animals.

I have achieved great success with my career, which is a major part of my life. I am in the rare situation of holding a senior executive position, which would normally be reserved for a man, in a very male-controlled industry.

For the last few years I have put my main energies into my work. It is an open secret in my circles of friends, work and business life that I am a lesbian.

I have not come out publicly for my own personal reasons. My choice has more to do with the fact that I am a very private person and quite shy and of course in part my decision reflects the fear and loss which I have experienced. If I came out publicly I feel I would have a duty to become a spokeswoman for lesbians and gays to try and help heterosexuals to understand the cloak of silence under which society still forces us to conduct our personal lives. I do not believe that I am the best person to do this. My skills are more suited to helping to change public opiinion by working behind the scenes rather than being a front person.

Over the years I have worked with gay and straight people and felt very uncomfortable about my sexuality mostly around 'right on', 'PC' or 'uptight' gays and liberal 'straights'. Now I enjoy the fact that all the people I choose to work with are straight and all of them know I am a lesbian and they really don't care, it does not bother them at all, and this gives me the greatest pleasure and peace of mind. All of the people that matter to me know about me. I take great satisfaction from this and from the people who work with and around me, and from my work where I know I have made major impacts.

CARMEL

I am twenty-three years old and come from a small village in Mayo. My father is a civil servant, and I have two brothers and a sister. I was educated at a community school which was primarily Catholic.

I came out to my parents when I was nineteen. They were both very upset, and my mother was quite hysterical. She felt that I was too young for such things, and that my being a lesbian would ruin my father's career. She also thought that some other woman had put me up to it (I was involved with another woman at the time).

My first lesbian relationship was when I was fifteen. It lasted for eight months. My partner was killed in a swimming accident when I was on holiday; by the time I returned home she was dead and buried. That was an awful time for me. It's a big thing in a small village, when a young person dies. I felt hysterical inside, but I could talk to no one about my grief. I just had to get on with life. I used to come home and cry every day, and always on my own.

When I was seventeen I moved to Dublin to go to college. I found a flat, and enjoyed making a new life for myself, with new friends. I made no contact with the gay community in Dublin, largely because I didn't know it existed. I found a part-time job in a restaurant and I met some gay people there. When I came across a gay newspaper in college, it seemed natural to me to read it. I found a phone number of a lesbian line, and I called them.

From this I went to a lesbian discussion group, where I met other gay people around my own age. I got to know more about the gay community and I learned a lot about myself. Over the next year or so I went out with a few people. I came out to my friends at college and had no problem there. Everyone was fine.

My parents, however, took me to a psychiatrist. They thought that I had problems and that I needed help. The psychiatrist was very good and in no way homophobic, and was actually very helpful to me. However, she didn't manage to console my mother.

I have always kept in touch with my parents. Things have been difficult. They will talk to me about my work, and where I live and so on, but they will not talk about my sexuality.

I've never come across prejudice in college or in my work. I don't live a double life. I have no qualms about having a social life on the gay scene. I've never hidden the fact that I'm a lesbian. It's so normal to me, and I am very comfortable with it.

I'm not presently in a relationship. I wouldn't go out with someone just for the sake of it. I'm not actively looking for a partner.

I would have left my village anyway – most young people do. I felt that I didn't fit in with the narrow attitudes, and there was so little to do there.

Today I help out at a bar for women. It's a place to socialise, where there's dancing, a bar and a restaurant. It's usually crowded and there's a wide range of women, of all ages and from all backgrounds.

CHRISTOPHER ROBSON

I'm a middle-aged, middle-class architect and have been living with my partner Bill for sixteen years. It took me forever to realise that I was gay, and then to accept it. I had a very confused period when I was falling in love with male friends and at the same time falling in love with male friends and at the same time attempting heterosexual relationships which at times were sexual; I liked, and like, women very much but never could fall in love with them.

I had been living as a gay man only for about three years when I met Bill, and hadn't really had many relationships. However, neither of us told our parents until we had been living together for some years. They thought he was essentially my lodger, and it is rather odd that it never occurred to either of the families what the truth of the situation was. My mother probably understood, but the revelation came as a real surprise to Bill's parents. His mother was very upset but always accepting. I grew to love her very much. Bill's father found it a little more difficult but I am now very good friends with him and with Bill's many brothers and sisters.

I didn't come out to the world at large until about 1983, when I became publicly involved with Gay Health Action, Ireland's first AIDS group. I realised that if I was going to speak for the group I would have to identify myself. It was when I told my eight-year-old niece that I realised that I was now hiding from nobody. I found it an enormous liberation and I would tell any gay person who isn't out to come out if it is at all possible. The sense of liberation and happiness at not being constantly in hiding is huge, and of enormous psychological benefit. The next advance in gay rights will only come out if all gay people are upfront about their sexuality and act together. I would like to see the high-level journalists and politicians, whom everybody knows about on a gossipy level, come out. The closet is a very damaging place to be and you are constantly under threat. Chris Smith, Labour MP for Islington in

London, is the only out MP in the House of Commons, and has publicly said that being out is liberating – everybody knows about him, so nobody cares.

Bill and I are in a successful long-term relationship because there is a great deal of shared love and affection between us – we have similar interests and sense of humour. However, I am concerned that this type of relationship, while it works for us, should not be held up as some kind of idealised norm. The notion of sexual fidelity derives almost entirely from children, and the paternity of those children, and the stability of the relationship in which those children are brought up. In gay and lesbian relationships fidelity is negotiated – if they are fully agreed to, open relationships are just as valid as permanent commitments. I feel that the nature of all relationships, gay and straight, is changing now, and that one of the ways in which gays have constructed relationships which is a real advance is in the notion of sexual friendships – relationships which are primarily friendships but which can occasionally include a sexual element. I feel that as long as the relationship – whether it be permanent or just for the weekend – is good for both partners, it is a valid relationship and can bring a sense of liberation and happiness.

Another way that relationship patterns, gay and straight, are changing is in the area of equality. There is a stereotype of gay couples consisting of a 'husband' and a 'wife', but it's not something I've ever come across. Even in heterosexual relationships the notion of sex-defined roles is becoming less and less obvious.

However, I do think gay relationships can be more difficult. It's a relatively new way of living, and people are not only having to enter patterns of life but to of models for heterosexual relationships do not exist for lesbians and gay men, and it can be a great shame if people think that their only hope of happiness is to find the right person and expect that relationship to solve all their problems. Because of this I feel that it's crucial for gay and lesbian couples to keep as strong a connection as possible to the gay community – it's very easy to drop out when you find a partner and then to find that when the relationship ends you're cut off from the support that the community brings.

I believe that lesbians and gay men have a responsibility to foster the gay community. Bill and I are deeply involved in activism and politics, and that's the context in which we live.

PART 3

Contacts

In this section you will find a list of helplines and useful addresses. These groups and lines have been established for the benefit of the enquirer – in other words, you. They can be of great help in answering any questions you may have or helping to allay any worries. It can often be a great relief simply to know that you are not alone. If you feel ill at ease contacting a lesbian or gay organisation, consider talking to the Samaritans, your family GP or a trained counsellor. The Samaritans can be found in your telephone directory, and for a qualified counsellor contact the Irish Association for Counselling on (01) 278 0411 or the British Associaton for Counselling on (0788) 550899.

IRELAND

NATIONAL ORGANISATIONS

Body Positive
Dame House,
24-26 Dame Street,
Dublin 2
(01) 671 2363/4
Self-help and support
group for people
affected by HIV or AIDS.

Employment Equality Agency (EEA)
36 Upr Mount Street,
Dublin 2
(01) 660 5966
Deals with cases of job
discrimination.

Gaeilgeori Aerach Aontaithe
(Irish-speaking gay group)
Roy Ó Gealbhain
Ionad Hirschfield
10 Sraid Fobhnais, BAC 2
(01) 671 0939

GLEN (Gay & Lesbian Equality Network)
c/o Hirschfeld Centre,
10 Fownes Street, Dublin 2
(01) 671 0939 (12.00-5.30pm)
Group lobbying for law
reform.

Irish Congress of Trade Unions (ICTU)
19 Raglan Road, Dublin 4
(01) 668 0641
Free policy document on
lesbian & gay rights in the
workplace.

Irish Council for Civil Liberties (ICCL)
35 Arran Quay, Dublin 1
(01) 873 4412

Irish Names Quilt
53 Parnell Square, Dublin 1
(01) 873 3799
Commemorative project for
those who have died of
AIDS.

Parents Enquiry
Carmichael House
North Brunswick Street
Dublin 7
(01) 872 1055
Support and information
for and by parents of
lesbians and gays.

LOCAL GROUPS

DUBLIN
AIDS Helpline Dublin
(01) 872 4277
Mon-Fri 7-9pm; Sat 3-5 pm

127

Alcholics Anonymous (AA)
Phone Lesbian Line or Gay Switchboard Dublin for details. Meets Monday 8pm.

Baggot Street Clinic
19 Haddington Road
Dublin 4
(01) 660 2149
Advice, counselling and HIV testing.

Cáirde
25 Mary's Abbey, Dublin 7
(01) 873 0006
Support for people affected by HIV or AIDS.

Dublin AIDS Alliance
53 Parnell Square, Dublin 1
(01) 873 3799

Dublin City University Lesbian & Gay Society
c/o Students Union Office DCU
Meets Thursdays 6pm.

First Out
c/o Lesbian Line or Gay Switchboard
Confidential support group for women exploring their sexuality, discussion facilitated by trained volunteers. Meets 1st Wednesday and 3rd Saturday each month at 7.30 pm.

Gay and Lesbian Counselling Service
(01) 8486291
Confidential one-to-one and couple counselling in the areas of sexual abuse, depression, coming out, relationships in conflict and self-development. Fully qualified counsellor.

Gay Men's Health Project
Baggot Street Clinic
(01) 660 2149
Tues & Wed 8.00-9.00pm
Drop-in centre – no appointment needed.

Gay Switchboard Dublin (GSD)
Carmichael House, North Brunswick Street, Dublin 7
(01) 872 1055
Sun-Fri 8-10pm
Sat. 3.30-6pm

Hirschfield Outdoors Group
10 Fownes Street, Dublin 2
(01) 671 0939
Meets last Sunday of the month at 11am.

Holistic Health Project
c/o Dublin AIDS
Alliance
(01) 873 3799
Massage, shiatsu and
relaxation sessions for
people affected by HIV or
AIDS.

Icebreakers
Contact Gay Switchboard,
Dublin
Informal meeting for gays
and lesbians coming out.
Meets 1st Saturday every
month in a city-centre hotel
at 7.30 pm.

Julian Fellowship
(01) 492 2843
Support and self-
development for Christian
lesbian women.
1st and last Thursday of
every month, 7.30-9pm.

**Kevin Street College
Lesbian and Gay Society**
c/o Students Union.
Meets every 2nd
Wednesday.

Lesbian Line
(01) 661 3777
Thurs 7-9pm

**LOT (Lesbians Organising
Together)**
5/6 Capel Street, Dublin 1
(01) 872 7770
Umbrella organisation
working in the fields of
health, publishing, LEN
(lesbian equality network),
social and entertainments
group, Frontline Services
(First Out and Dublin
Lesbian Line) providing
advice, support and
information and referrals.
Regular meetings on the
first Thursday of the
month.

**NLGF (National Lesbian
& Gay Federation)**
The Hirschfield Centre, 10
Fownes Street, Dublin 2
(01) 671 2363/4

**Metropolitan Community
Church**
(01) 857 403
American-oriented gay-
and lesbian-friendly
Christian church.

**Muted Cupid Theatre
Group**
Upstairs Rumpoles Bar
Parliament Street, Dublin 2
Meets Tuesdays, 7.30 pm.

Reach
PO Box 1790, Dublin 6
(01) 492 2843
Gay Christian group. Meets
monthly on Saturday in
Dublin.

**St James' Hospital GU
Clinic**
Hospital 5, Rialto Entrance,
Dublin 8
(01) 453 5245
(01) 453 7941 ext. 2315/16
Mon & Fri 9-12.30pm
Tue & Thur 1.30-4.30pm
HIV Clinic
(01) 453 5245
(01) 453 7941 ext. 2161
Mon 1.30-4.30pm
Wed 9-12pm

**TCD Lesbian, Gay and Bi
Society**
Meets Room 6.26,
Thursdays at 7.30 pm

Youth Group Dublin
Details from Gay
Switchboard.
Social group of under-25s,
meeting the first and third
Sunday of the month.

**BELFAST
Carefriend**
(0232) 322 023 Mon-Wed
7.30-10 pm

Counselling and befriend-
ing service for gay men.

Gay Christian Fellowship
Cathedral Building
PO Box 44
Belfast BT1 1SH
Meets 2nd and 4th Sun at
3pm in Cathedral Building,
64 Donegal Street.

Lesbian and Gay Line NW
PO Box 44
Belfast BT1 1SH
(0504) 263 120

Lesbian Line
(0232) 322 023
Thurs 7.30-10 pm
Counselling and
befriending service for
lesbians.

**NIGRA (Northern Ireland
Gay Rights Association)**
PO Box 44, Belfast BT1 1SH
(0232) 664 111/325851

Parents Enquiry
(0232) 466 944
Fri, `Mon 7:30 – 10:00 pm.

**CORK
Alcoholics Anonymous**
Contact Lesbian Line or
Gay Information

AIDS Helpline Cork
(021) 276 676
Mon-Fri 10 am-5 pm

Cork Gay Collective
Icebreakers
Meets last Tuesday of the
month at 8pm.
Contact Lesbian/Gay Line
for details.

Cork Lesbian Line
(021) 27 10 87
Thurs 8-10pm

Gay Information Cork
(021) 27 10 87
Wed 7-9pm
Sat 3-5 pm

**Lesbian and Gay Resource
Group**
The Other Place, 7/8
Augustine Street
(021) 317 660

Reach
PO Box 1790
Dublin 6
(021) 291 371
Gay Christian group.

STD Clinic
Victoria Hospital
Monday 5.30-7.30 pm
Wed 10-12 pm

DERRY
Derry Lesbian Line
(0504) 26 31 20
Thursdays 7.30-10pm
Drop-In Centre
Women's Centre
London Street
Sat 2.30 – 4.30pm

Icebreakers
Top Floor,
37 Clarendon Street
Meetings for young
lesbians just coming out,
every Wednesday evening.

DROGHEDA (LOUTH)
Outcomes
c/o Resource Centre for the
Unemployed
7 North Quay
Drogheda
Social group for gay men
and lesbians, meeting on
the second and fourth
Friday of each month.
Contact Gay Switchboard
Dublin for information.

GALWAY
AIDS Help West
Ozanam House
(091) 66266
Mon-Fri 10-12 pm
Thurs 8-10 pm

Galway Gay Help Line
PO Box 45
(091) 66134
Tues and Thurs 8-10 pm

Galway Lesbian Line
PO Box 45
(091) 66134
Wed 8-10 pm

Parents Enquiry
(091) 66134
Information service and
helpline for parents of
lesbians and gay men.

PLUTO
UCG Lesbian Gay and Bi
Group
Details from Gay/Lesbian
Line.

KERRY
Tralee
(066) 6710939
Meets Tues and 4th Friday

LIMERICK
Gay Switchboard
Limerick
(061) 310101
Mon, Tues 7.30-9.30 pm

Lesbian Line
(061) 310101
Thurs 7.30-9.30 pm

Limerick AIDS Alliance
PO Box 103, Cecil Street

Limerick AIDS Helpline
(061) 316661
Mon/Thurs 7.30 – 9.30pm

Limerick Forum
Details from Gay Switch-
board. Social meetings for
gays, lesbians and bisexuals.
Meets every second
Wednesday 8.30 pm.

SLIGO
**Gala (Gay and Lesbian
Association)**
c/o Hirschfield Centre

WATERFORD
**Lesbian and Gay Line
South East**
(051) 79907
Lesbian line
Mon 7.30-9.30 pm
Gay line
Wed 7.30-9.30

Parents Enquiry
(051) 79907
Mon, Wed 7.30-9.30 pm

Waterford Assembly
PO Box 24, GPO
(051) 6710939
Social group meeting on first
Saturday of the month.

ENGLAND

LONDON
**AIDS Care Education
Project,** Queen's Hospital
Queen's Road
Croydon
Surrey.
Sonia (081) 665 5000
Support group for family
and friends of people with
AIDS. Monday to Friday 9-
5 pm.

**Cáirde – London Friend
Women's Helpline**
86 Caledonian Road,
London N1
(071) 837 2782/837 3337
Social and support group
for Irish lesbians, meeting
7.30-10 pm every evening.

Irish Gay Helpline
(081) 983 4111
Information and
befriending service.
Mon 7.30 – 10pm.

**Lesbian and Gay Christian
Movement**
Oxford House, Derbyshire
Street, London E2 6HG
(071) 587 1235
Runs a helpline, Sun and
Wed, 7-10 pm.

**Lesbian/Gay Switchboard
London**
(071) 837 7324
24-hour service, seven days
a week.

**Parents and Friends of
Lesbians and Gays**
(081) 523 2910
(ask for Eve).

Parents Enquiry
Rose Robertson
16 Honley Road
London SE6 2H2
(081) 698 1815.

**Positively Irish Action on
AIDS**
21 Old Ford Road
London E2 9PL
Advice, information and
referral service.

**Quaker Lesbian and Gay
Fellowship**
Contact Ruth, GCN
3 Hallsfield, Cricklade
Swindon, Hertfordshire.

BIRMINGHAM
AIDS Information
(021) 212 3636

Gay Switchboard
(021) 6336589

BLACKPOOL
AIDS Information
(0253) 408 520

Gay Switchboard
(0253) 752105

BOURNEMOUTH
Gay Switchboard
(0202) 318822

BRIGHTON
AIDS Information
(0273) 561 770

Gay Switchboard
(0273) 690825

KENT
Kent Parents Enquiry
(0795) 661 463 (Jill Green)

LEICESTER
Leicester Parents Group
(0533) 550667
Mon-Fri 7.30-10 pm

MANCHESTER
AIDS Information
(061) 228 1617

Manchester Gay Group
(061) 274 3814

YORK
AIDS Information
(0904) 620 520

Gay Switchboard
(0894) 411399

SCOTLAND

EDINBURGH
Lesbian Line
(031) 557 0751
Mon-Thurs
7.30-10 pm

Scottish Parents Enquiry
c/o Gay Switchboard
PO Box 164, Edinburgh
(031) 5564049
Thurs 7.30-10 pm

Stonewall Youth Group
(031) 556 4040
Meeting for young gay
men, every Tues 7.30-9 pm

GLASGOW
Gay Switchboard
(041) 2218372

WALES

CARDIFF
AIDS Information
(0222) 223 443

Gay Switchboard
(0222) 340101

Selected Reading

You may find the following books useful or informative. Some are practical; some are novels which give an interesting perspective. Try your library too.

A Stranger in the Family Terry Sanderson, The Other Way Press, 1991
An excellent guide to coming to terms with your child's homosexuality.

When Love Comes to Town Tom Lennon, O'Brien Press, 1993

My Parents Hervé Gurbert, Serpent's Tail, 1986

Assertively Gay Terry Sanderson, The Other Way Press, 1993

The Lost Language of Cranes David Leavitt, Penguin, 1986
An extremely moving novel of a young man's coming out to his parents.

Young, Gay and Proud Ed. Sasha Alyson, Alyson Publishing, 1990

Dancing on the Moon Jameson Currier, Penguin, 1991

Lesbian Women Martin & Lyon, Volcano Press, 1992

The Guide to Lesbian and Gay Parenting April Martin, Pandora, 1993

The Alternative Ireland Directory Quay Co-op, 1990

Diverse Communities Kieran Rose, Cork University
    Press, 1994

Hidden From History: Reclaiming the gay and lesbian past
    M. B. Duberman *et al.*, eds., Penguin, 1991

Safety in Numbers: Safe sex and gay men E. King, Cassell,
    1993

A Priest on Trial Bernard Lynch, Bloomsbury, 1993

Of Woman Born: Motherhood as experience and institution
    Adrienne Rich, Virago, 1977

Quare Fellas: New Irish Gay Writing Brian Finnegan ed.,
    Basement Press, 1984

The Kiss Linda Cullen, Attic Press, 1988

Magazines

Gay Community News
10 Fownes Street, Dublin 2
(01) 671 0939
Free monthly newspaper for Irish gays and lesbians.
Keeps the gay community up to date with important
issues and also features a complete list of all Ireland's
gay venues.

Gay Times
A monthly British publication covering current affairs,
entertainment and lifestyles, and available from many
newsagents and bookstalls.

Gemma
PO Box 5700, London WC1N 3XX
Quarterly newsletter for lesbian and bi-sexual women
of all ages, with or without disabilities.

Our View
Concentrates on news and current affairs from a gay
and lesbian perspective. Available in bookshops.

In London a wide range of gay newspapers and
magazines is available, most of them distributed free in
bars and clubs. These include *The Pink Paper*, *Boyz* and
many others.

Irish Congress of Trade Unions Guidelines for Lesbian and Gay Rights in the Workplace

---

- Lesbians and gay men are women and men whose most important relationships are with other women and other men.
- There are lesbians and gays in all social classes, in all age groups, and in all parts of the country.
- It is a common mistake to believe that these people are few, and there are none where we work. Research many years ago showed that one person in ten is predominantly lesbian or gay. This figure when applied to Ireland would amount to over 300,000 men and women – perhaps the largest minority in the country. In a workforce of a hundred, some ten people may be lesbian or gay.

- Many lesbians and gay men are denied the basic right to work as they are often refused jobs solely on grounds of their sexuality.
- At work, lesbians and gays are often afraid of the opinions of their colleagues. They are afraid that if their sexuality becomes known they will lose any chance of promotion, and above all, they are afraid of losing their jobs.
- The enforced secrecy about people's lives is damaging, and the continuous necessity to lie or pretend can cause isolation, mental stress and alcoholic problems.
- Discrimination also occurs in relation to conditions of employment. Pensions and benefits are paid for, but cannot be passed on to partners.

    Lesbian and gay workers are often subjected to harassment from management and co-workers. Harassment can broadly be described as persistent, unwanted behaviour intended to humiliate a person. This can take the form of personal questions, offensive jokes, innuendo and malicious gossip. A lesbian or gay worker may be isolated by co-workers. In extreme cases a person may be physically attacked. The labour court has stated that freedom from sexual harassment is a condition of work which an employee of either sex is entitled to expect.

- Anti-lesbian and gay prejudice often focuses on certain work areas, particularly those which involve young people. Discrimination in those areas is very often exercised at the recruitment and selection stage.
- Complaints or grievances in relation to discrimination agains lesbian and gay workers arise mainly in relation to recruitment, promotion and training

harassment, conditions of employment.

- Lesbian and gay workers may be reluctant to openly state that the complaint or grievance is related to their sexuality, as they might fear that this would endanger their jobs. On the other hand, management will usually try to hide or deny that they have discriminated against workers because of their sexuality, or in response to other people's prejudices, and they will try to put it in other terms such, as a 'personality clash'.

- Lesbian and gay workers should be able to raise any of these issues with their union representative and expect it to be dealt with in a positive and supportive manner. Trade union representatives need to be sensitive to the nature and scope of the discrimination which may occur.

Glossary

ACTIVISTS: Lesbian and gay activists are people who work to gain recognition for or protection of lesbian and gay rights.

AIDS: Acquired Immune Deficiency syndrome. People do not die of AIDS. A person with AIDS (sometimes referred to as PWA) might however succumb to diseases or infections they are unable to overcome due to a failed immune system.

CAMP: This can refer to anything humorously or outrageously 'over the top', for example, flamboyant activity, clothing or decor.

CLOSET: 'Closets are for clothes' is a familiar lesbian and gay saying. 'Being in the closet' is a euphemism for living in fear of your sexuality or hiding it from others.

COMING OUT: Coming out is leaving the closet behind. It is the process where lesbians and gay men overcome their fear and come out of hiding. It involves accepting one's homosexuality and learning to live with that within our society and learning to live with and share that acceptance with family and friends. In the USA there is a National Coming Out Day on October 11.

CRUISING: This is a term typical to gay men, to describe the process of looking for and approaching people to whom they are attracted.

DYKE: Once a term of abuse to describe lesbians, though now lesbians often refer to themselves as dykes.

FAGGOT: One of the many terms of abuse applied to gay men. Others include poofter, pansy, nancy boy, shirt lifter and many more.

GAY-BASHING: Physically or verbally abusing a lesbian or gay person because of their sexuality. Sometimes any form of lesbian and gay discrimination is referred to as gay bashing.

GAY GAMES: An event like the Olympic Games which takes place every four years. Organised by the lesbian and gay community it is open to everyone regardless of sexual orientation. World records have been set at these games and thousands of top-class athletes participate. In 1996 the Gay Games will be held in Amsterdam.

GAY PRIDE/EURO PRIDE/GAY MARDI GRAS: Every year, generally in June, most urban centres across the world with a lesbian and gay population will be treated to a Gay Pride Parade. Euro Pride is a joyous celebration of being 'Out, Loud and Proud' and takes place at a different European city each year. Gay Mardi Gras is

Sydney's enormous celebration of lesbian strength and gay pride. In Ireland the lesbian and gay communities of Cork, Belfast, Galway, Dublin and Drogheda have organised Gay Pride parades and festivals.

HIV: The virus which can lead to a weakening of the immune system and a development of AIDS.

HOMOPHOBIA: Fear, dislike or disgust of homosexuality. People who cannot accept homosexuality are homophobic.

LESBIAN AND GAY COMMUNITY: The social, cultural and political support network of lesbians and gay men.

LESBIAN LINE/GAY SWITCHBOARD: A telephone helpline for people who are having difficulty with work, home or coming out. Operated on a voluntary basis, it is also an information line regarding upcoming events within the community.

LESBIAN SEPARATISM: A political philosophy developed in the 1970s which advocates that lesbians' priorities should lie with working and interacting with lesbians only.

QUEEN: A flamboyant gay man.

QUEER: Formerly a term of abuse directed at lesbians and gay men, 'queer' has become associated with a political enterprise which advocates that lesbians and gay men work together in philosophising about their lives and culture (Queer Theory) and engaging together in public campaigns and direct action (Queer Politics).

THE SCENE: A collective term for lesbian and gay facilities – for example bars, clubs and meeting places.

TRANSSEXUAL: Someone who feels that they are in the wrong body for their sex. For instance, someone with all the appearances of a man may feel very strongly that he is a woman in the wrong body and may have an operation to 'become' a woman. Although some transsexuals may have relationships with members of their own sex, it is a common mistake to believe that they are homosexual. Lesbians or gay men are very happy as women or men and do not want to change.

TRANSVESTITE: Almost inevitably a heterosexual man who enjoys wearing women's clothes for sexual pleasure. A common misconception is that transvestites are homosexual.